Valentina

An Odyssey from Pre-Revolutionary Russia Through War-Torn Europe to a Pacific Paradise

Emiko Lyovin

Order this book online at www.trafford.com
or email orders@trafford.com

Most Trafford titles are also available at major online book retailers.

© Copyright 2012, 2014 Emiko Lyovin.
All rights reserved. No part of this publication may be reproduced, stored in a retrieval system, or transmitted, in any form or by any means, electronic, mechanical, photocopying, recording, or otherwise, without the written prior permission of the author.

Printed in the United States of America.

ISBN: 978-1-4669-4433-6 (sc)
ISBN: 978-1-4669-4432-9 (hc)
ISBN: 978-1-4669-4431-2 (e)

Library of Congress Control Number: 2012913739

Trafford rev. 03/12/2014

 www.trafford.com

North America & international
toll-free: 1 888 232 4444 (USA & Canada)
fax: 812 355 4082

CONTENTS

Foreword v
Valentina Lyovin's Family Tree vii
Prologue ix

Part I **A Child of the Clergy**

Chapter 1 Proposal on Nevsky Prospect 1
Chapter 2 Birth and Death 9
Chapter 3 Pascha 16
Chapter 4 Tantochka's House 22
Chapter 5 Two Brothers 29
Chapter 6 A Sister 33
Chapter 7 Calf-Love 39
Chapter 8 Journey to Crimea 47

Part II **The Twilight of Imperial Russia**

Chapter 9   Petrograd 53
Chapter 10 Ideologues Flock Home 60
Chapter 11 Cousins 67
Chapter 12 Brother's Wife 73
Chapter 13 February Revolution 79

Part III **Fate Driven by Revolution**

Chapter 14 Ekaterinodar 86
Chapter 15 The Red Army 95

Chapter 16	Valentina Elopes	107
Chapter 17	Kharkov	114
Chapter 18	Amidst Civil War	135
Chapter 19	Novorossiysk	142
Chapter 20	Leaving Mother Russia	151

Part IV — From Nazism to Communism

Chapter 21	The First Foreign Land of Refuge	156
Chapter 22	Macedonia	165
Chapter 23	For Love or Money	171
Chapter 24	Dalmatia	177
Chapter 25	Under Nazi Occupation	188
Chapter 26	Belgrade	203
Chapter 27	Slovenia and Montenegro	213
Chapter 28	Leaving Yugoslavia	220

Part V — To the Land of Rest

Chapter 29	Refugees in Italy	228
Chapter 30	To Canada	236
Chapter 31	The New Member of the Family	243
Chapter 32	Valentina's Twilight Years	249

Epilogue	257
Acknowledgments	259
Bibliography	261
About the author	265

FOREWORD

This book is written in tribute to my mother-in-law, Valentina Valerianovna Lyovina, with whom I lived under the same roof for a period of some ten years beginning in 1968.

Her stories inspired me to share her life's adventures and life lessons with like-minded people. Valentina related the central events of her life to me during the ten-year interval when she lived with my husband, Anatole Lyovin, and me in Honolulu. She also handwrote a few of the many stories of her youth. I collected and collated the historical facts before I started writing her biography. I also interviewed the living relatives of Valentina to check their versions of her story and was amazed to find how accurate Valentina's memory had proven to be. The first version of this book was published in Japanese by Bungei Shunjū, Tokyo, Japan, in 1998. The English translation contains additional information about her later life.

I had been mulling over plans to write a chronicle of the life of Valentina for many years when the fall of the Soviet Union of 1991 convinced me that the hour of need had arrived.

When I told Valentina that I would like to write the story of her life, she talked freely and openly about everything she had a personal memory of or had been told. Because of her expansive character, there were some typically Russian exaggerations in some of the episodes and sometimes a second telling of a story would undergo changes. However, on the whole, her consistency and clarity of memory for details were impressive.

Although this account is intended to be rigorously factual, it was necessary to change some of the names in order to protect the privacy of individuals or, in the case of namesakes, to avoid confusion.

VALENTINA LYOVIN'S FAMILY TREE

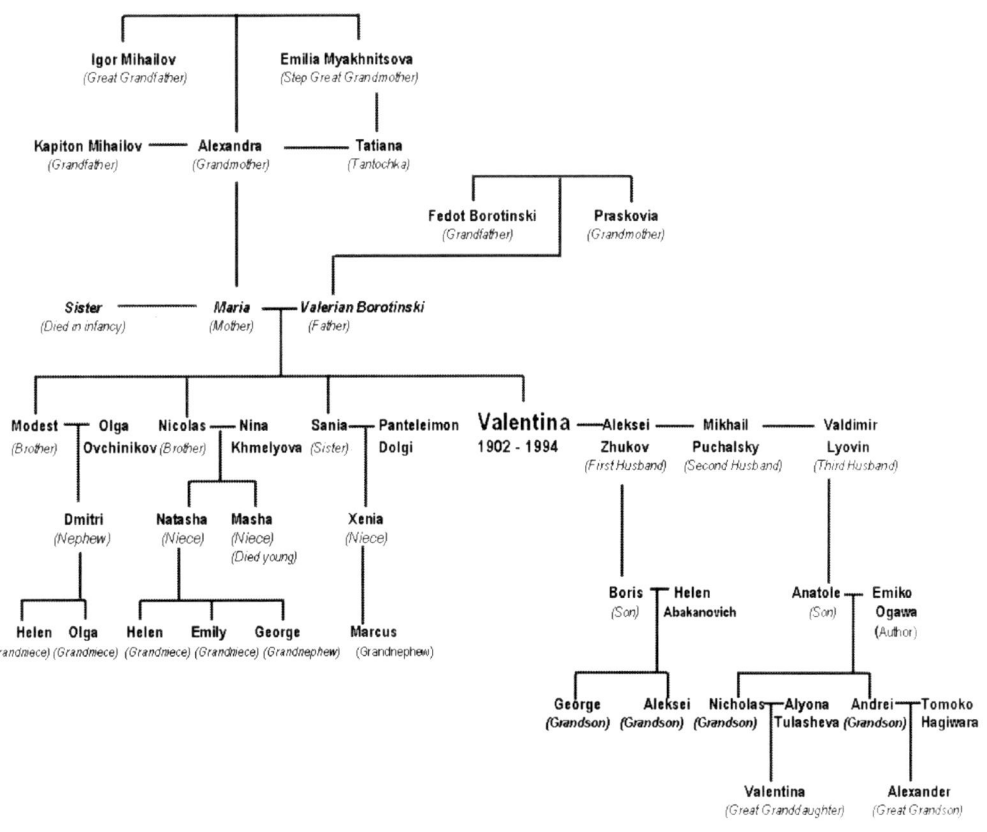

PROLOGUE

I am Emiko, daughter-in-law of Valentina. I arrived in San Francisco from Yokohama aboard the American President Line passenger ship *President Wilson* in May 1964. My future brother-in-law, Boris, bought my ticket. When I arrived at the San Francisco port and was waiting for the luggage to be disembarked, I heard someone behind me shout "Emiko, Emiko!" I turned around and saw two tall women in coats waving to me outside the gate. The older ash-blond one was Valentina, and the younger one was my future sister-in-law, Helen. I ran to greet them. Valentina said that she recognized me even from the back. We recognized each other from the frequent letters and pictures we had exchanged over the previous two years. Valentina captured my heart and imagination with her stately presence and beautiful warm smile.

I had met her son, Anatole, in 1962 when he visited Tokyo on his way to Taiwan. He was my pen pal from Princeton University. I had joined the International Amity Club at Sophia University in Tokyo, where I was a student. To promote international friendship, the members of the club were required to have at least one foreign pen pal. Out of the huge directory of American universities in the club office, I picked Princeton from among the Ivy League colleges. My letter requesting a pen pal had ended up in the hands of Professor

Valdo Viglielmo, a professor of Japanese Language and Literature at Princeton. He asked his Japanese class if anyone would be interested in corresponding with a Japanese girl. None among the four students who were studying Japanese language showed an interest. Professor Viglielmo was about to toss my letter into the wastepaper basket when one of his students, Anatole Lyovin from Canada, felt sorry for the girl and decided to reply to my letter. No sooner had we started corresponding than Anatole was offered a scholarship to study abroad for one year. He was assigned to study the Chinese language at Taiwan National University in Taipei. We had met in Tokyo in June 1962, during the rainy season. Although I was already promised to someone else, I soon fell in love with Anatole and broke up with my fiancé. Anatole proposed to me one week after we first met. What struck me about Anatole were his childlike innocence, his great intelligence, his gallantry, and his delightful sense of humor. To this day I think that my decision to marry him was the best thing I ever did in my life.

When I left Japan to marry Anatole, Valentina flew from Toronto to San Francisco. Her elder son Boris and his family had just moved to California from Michigan, and Valentina decided to visit Boris and meet me there at the same time. Boris's family welcomed me. He and his two teenage sons were over six feet tall. I felt like a dwarf surrounded by giants. I am only five feet tall.

Anatole and I were scheduled to marry in the Holy Trinity Russian Orthodox Church in Toronto on July 12, 1964, right after the Lent of Saint Peter and Saint Paul. Archbishop Vitaly of Montreal and Eastern Canada was to marry us. Valentina had arranged the catechumen class for me by the

Orthodox priest who became my godfather. I was baptized by Archbishop Vitaly the day before the wedding day.

After our honeymoon, we spent the rest of the summer with Anatole's parents, where I received a crash course in Russian cooking from Valentina. My father-in-law, Vladimir, worked the night shift at the hospital to support his family and pay for Anatole's education. When Vladimir left for his job at night, I noticed that no one saw him off at the front door. I was puzzled by this—after all, all his efforts were for his family and Anatole's education. I was moved by this show of selflessness and dedication, so I took to seeing him off each time he left for work. I wished him "good night" and kept the outside light on until he was out of sight. This apparently pleased my father-in-law greatly. Anatole later told me that he would often boast to his friends about the consideration with which his Japanese daughter-in-law treated him.

In another instance, while still in our honeymoon mood, I took to cutting my husband's toenails on my lap. Papa Vladimir saw this and told Anatole, "Your mom never did that for me. You married gold, Son." I was surprised to receive praise for doing something that I completely took for granted.

After leaving Toronto, we started our new life at Berkeley. Anatole continued his doctorate studies in linguistics in Berkeley, California. Then in 1965, our elder son Nicholas was born. Vladimir was overjoyed that he had a grandson. One day when I was fussing over our baby Nicholas, there was a phone call. I picked up the phone and heard "hello." I immediately recognized Vladimir's deep base voice. "Is that you, Papa?" No reply came, and the line went dead. The next day, we learned that Vladimir had passed away.

In 1968, we moved to Honolulu, and Anatole started teaching linguistics at the University of Hawaii. We invited Valentina to live with us. Valentina finally left her home in Toronto and moved to Honolulu to be with us. When we took her for a drive around the island of Oahu shortly after arriving, she marveled at the shape of the mountains. So different from the European Alps that she knew, Hawaii's jagged mountains seemed wild and exciting like the violent volcanic upheavals that had created them. On the windward side of the island, Valentina loved the way the Koolau Mountains towered in precipitous walls over the nearby valleys. The color of the ocean was also very different from the gray Baltic Sea of her childhood in St. Petersburg or from the dark blue of the Black Sea or the bright blue of the Adriatic Sea along the coast of Dubrovnik in Croatia. This Pacific Ocean surrounding Hawaii was an "almost translucent blue." She kept saying, "It feels like a different planet!"

Valentina seemed very happy to be with us, in particular, regarding her two grandsons, Nicholas and Andrei. "Hawaii is truly a paradise!" she wrote on postcard after postcard to her friends in Toronto.

Living with Valentina, however, was not always easy. She wanted to control everything in our life and gave her opinion on every matter. She also loved to talk to me endlessly about everything in her life. Although I liked listening to her stories, I had no time left for my housework. I began to feel suffocated with frustration. I often felt like screaming. After suffering in silence for a few months, I exploded, saying, "I don't want to go on living like this! I don't have my space in this house! We have to do something about this!" Valentina was startled to hear such words from her supposedly obedient Japanese daughter-in-law. I felt terrible about speaking my mind so rudely and angrily, and I decided that I would apologize to her. I had heard someone say, "It takes a big person to apologize." I mustered all the strength I could and apologized. Valentina, magnanimous and bigger than life, accepted my apology and openheartedly talked over what to do. The situation improved. Later, I started working as a part-time newscaster at the local Japanese radio station and later as a Japanese language teacher. Valentina also found things to do. She kept herself busy with oil painting, embroidering, gardening, and tutoring. Living with Valentina taught me many things about Russian culture, Russian cuisine, and the Russian Orthodox faith. She blanketed me with her affection for the rest of her life. Whatever our individual faults, we developed a mutual respect for each other. Despite an occasional cultural clash, we lived in harmony, and her presence enlightened me. I now relate her story to you with great tenderness and relish.

CHAPTER I

Proposal on Nevsky Prospect

Countless were the times that Valentina had heard from her parents the family legend of her paternal grandfather!

It went as follows: As the nineteenth century drew toward a close, Grandfather Fedot Ivanovich Borotinski had been, for some years, eking out a precarious living as a lector, or tonsured church reader, at a small Orthodox church in a shabby corner of the great city of St. Petersburg. At that time, St. Petersburg was the capital of the vast realm of Imperial Russia and had opened its window on the cultured nations of the West—in particular, France and Prussia. By all reports, Fedot was a good and guileless man. Yet despite his best efforts, it was increasingly difficult for him to feed and clothe his family of five sons and one daughter on his scant benefice alone.

One evening, at a time when they were feeling the bite of poverty most keenly, Fedot and his wife, Praskovia, sat up late casting about for a way out of their predicament, but they fell asleep without coming up with a single practical solution. The night deepened. Suddenly, the bedroom door flew open, and in bustled a stranger wearing an overcoat and carrying his hat in hand. Without a word, he drew a chair up close to the astounded couple's bed and in a low voice began to speak. "First thing tomorrow morning," he said, "write out a request to serve at the Uspensky Church in Sennaya Square. Take it there yourself. You must go in person." Then, without uttering another word, he rose to his feet, and just as suddenly as he had arrived, their visitor turned and left. A mystified Fedot immediately rose and went to the front door, only to find it securely locked from the inside. Someone would have had to let the stranger in, but the children were all sound asleep.

The next morning, he questioned the entire household, but no one had heard the bell ring or the front door open.

How bizarre! he thought. Even so, Fedot decided to follow to the instructions given by his mysterious midnight caller. He set out, petition in hand, for the great Uspensky Church, fondly referred to by the people of St. Petersburg as the Sennaya Savior. To Fedot's surprise, when he arrived, he was informed that three days earlier, one of the church's readers had died. He was offered the job. This is the family story that explains how Fedot found employment in the great church in Sennaya Square, saving them all from abject poverty.

Fedot had five sons and one daughter. It was long the custom in Russia for the sons of priests to receive their schooling at a seminary while their daughters attended a boarding school run by the church. No fee was charged for their education. In most cases, sons married the offspring of other clergymen and succeeded to their father or father-in-law's position in the church. Following his father's footsteps, Valerian, Valentina's father, also answered the call to the religious service and became a Russian Orthodox priest. However, he did not conform to the custom of marrying a priest's daughter. Instead, he fell in love with and married a distant cousin who attended his father's church in Sennaya Square. As the girl was not the daughter of a cleric, Valerian's mother, in particular, was stubbornly opposed to the match. However, Valerian refused to yield, and in the end, the family received into their midst Maria Kapitonovna, who was not a child of the church. Valerian's mother forever regretted her lapse of parental rigor. Whenever a problem arose concerning this marriage, she would say, "After all, what can you expect? She isn't one of us." Although Maria was an outsider to this family of clerics, she came from a highly respected family and was by no means their social inferior. Her grandfather, Igor Myakhnitsov, was a handsome and cultured son of a government official who steadily rose in the government circles and won entrée to St. Petersburg's polite society. Through these connections, he met and married Emilia, the daughter of an impoverished but distinguished aristocratic family. Emilia was Igor's second wife, his first having died shortly after giving birth to a daughter, Alexandra. Unlike the wicked stepmother of Russian folktales, Emilia tenderly took the stepdaughter under her wing. From the start, the marriage was a happy one, and the couple was soon blessed with another daughter, whom they named Tatiana. But fate dealt them a cruel blow when, after an agonizing struggle with cancer, Igor died at the young age of thirty-nine, leaving his widow Emilia with two daughters, a small pension, and meager savings.

As luck would have it, when Tsar Alexander II was struck down by an assassin's bomb on March 1, 1881, his consort automatically became the Dowager Empress Maria Alexandrovna. A woman of strong charitable instincts,

Dowager Empress Maria took into her service a young noblewoman, Ekaterina, who had been orphaned when her parents' ship went down at sea on its way to the United States. And it was as a companion to Ekaterina, lady-in-waiting to the Dowager Empress, that the widowed Emilia entered into service. This enabled her stepdaughter Alexandra to grow up in the shadows—in an atmosphere of royalty.

Alexandra was tall and skinny and wore glasses. When she approached marriageable age, the brother of a classmate, Kapiton, expressed interest in the lanky, intelligent girl and sought her hand in marriage. Her stepmother agreed. After a small wedding ceremony, the new couple left St. Petersburg for Perm, a city located in the cold, harsh provinces of the Ural Mountains, where Kapiton was to take up a position as a mining engineer.

Their first child, a girl, died at birth, but their second, Maria, was a healthy girl on whom they lavished their affections and spared no effort in her upbringing. Despite the harsh climate of the Urals, young Maria thrived. She grew to become a clever girl with an independent mind. Friendly and bright, she was ever popular with her classmates. Maria was also blessed with a good retentive memory, allowing her to pick up new words and concepts with great ease. Consequently, her favorite subjects in school were foreign languages, in which she excelled.

The years passed happily and uneventfully until one day, when Maria was in her final year of high school, tragedy struck. There was a terrible cave-in at the mines, and a number of miners, including the engineers, lost their lives. Maria's father was one of them. Maria and her mother were in despair. To whom could they turn? Alexandra wrote to her stepsister Tatiana, inquiring of her stepmother Emilia and the companion to Lady Ekaterina in St. Petersburg. She learned that Lady Ekaterina was now married, and since the marriage, her stepmother Emilia had been offered a new position as supervisor of servants. Emilia felt that the job was demeaning to one who had walked the same corridors as Tsar Alexander III himself. In her bitterness, Emilia aired constant complaints to Tatiana, and unable to bear her mother's daily groans, Tatiana now considered leaving her mother for lodgings of her own.

Under such circumstances, Alexandra could not count on the likelihood that her stepmother would cheerfully take her in. She decided instead to prevail upon an old friend, who then found a small apartment for her and her daughter in St. Petersburg. Maria arrived in the capital with her mother in 1892. She was sixteen years old.

Tsar Alexander III had become tsar in 1881 following the assassination of his father Alexander II. By now, Alexander III had become unable to contain the rising tide of political activism. History records the irony that among the five conspirators who were summarily executed after a plot to kill Alexander III was uncovered in 1887 was Alexander Ulyanov, brother of Vladimir Ilyich Ulyanov, the future Bolshevik V. I. Lenin.

St. Petersburg was a great metropolis crisscrossed by a network of canals. It had a population of 1.4 million people and bore the proud epithet "Venice of the North." Gazing at last upon the capital city where her mother was born, young Maria's eyes flooded with tears. She doubted there could be any other place in the world as beautiful.

She was especially moved by the beauty of the panoramic view of the city across the Great Neva from the Vasilievsky Island. She could see the Admiralty, the elegant Winter Palace and St. Isaac's Cathedral with its soaring steeples. Nevsky Prospect was lined with fine shops, in whose windows luxury goods were on display for all to see, if not to buy. She had heard of these places from her mother, but to be actually in their midst seemed a dream come true, and she vowed that she would never leave this city.

Life in St. Petersburg was daunting for a girl newly arrived from the provinces with no special skills and with no friends. It was an era when a woman, unless she had a specialized education, would have had great difficulty in finding work. Other than schoolteacher, governess, or nurse, there were few occupations available in the late nineteenth century that would enable a woman to support herself. The time was drawing near when Maria would have had to make decisions about her future. The clear-headed and studious Maria wanted to continue with school, but her mother could barely pay the rent and buy food, let alone pay for her daughter's studies! In light of the reality of the poverty of their situation, education was out of reach to the aspiring Maria.

Alexandra was troubled by her daughter's plight. It saddened her to see her daughter always engrossed in a book or walking along the broad avenues of the city in quiet solitude. It seemed her agile minded daughter longed for something more than she could provide. One day, as Maria strolled quietly along Nevsky Prospect, St. Petersburg's grandest promenade, a voice called out to her. It was Valerian Fedotovich Borotinski, a young seminary student and distant cousin whom she had met at church. Maria's cheeks flushed bright red, for she had never before been spoken to on the streets, much less by a man. Soon her solitary strolls were replaced by long rambles with Valerian, during which they shared with each other thoughts and visions of what the future held for them.

Valerian, who was about to graduate from seminary, wanted to follow his father into the church. He dreamed of becoming a priest at a big church in St. Petersburg. To do this, he required further training. To avoid placing a financial burden on his frugal parents, he planned to find a position at a small church first and, in this way, fund his own way through his studies. He was looking for something in an outlying town or at a chapel attached to a boarding school or orphanage. This way, he could continue his studies at St. Petersburg Theological Academy.

Besides being a good-looking man, Valerian was a kindhearted young man with a lively sense of humor. His witty stories often drew giggles from the serious-minded Maria. There was one story, in particular, however, that Maria especially liked. It was a story he told of how he came to pursue the life of a priest.

Valerian and all his brothers attended gymnasium as boys, and though they all earned passing grades, Valerian's grades were notably the worst. Once, having received his poor report card, he sat aboard a small boat that ferried passengers across the Neva River. In the late nineteenth century, there were few bridges to allow for the crossing of the river by foot, and so the ferry was the normal mode of crossing. Here Valerian conceived of a grand idea: He would discard his report card with all the poor marks into the waters of the Neva River. Unfortunately for him, the report card refused to sink but floated on the surface until it finally reached the shore. A conscientious do-gooder, passing by and seeing the report card lying on the river's shore, picked it up and promptly took it to the school. In the end, Valerian was forced to confess his prank. When the principal told Valerian's father about his son's attempt to discard of the report card, his father began to cry. Those tears had a strange effect on Valerian. He had expected anger, punishment—anything but tears from his father! Valerian was so shaken that he felt moved to redirect his life. He chose religion. He pleaded with his father to let him transfer to a seminary. He also promised to become a better student in the future.

Valerian's witty stories gradually gave way to more serious matters as he deepened in his love for Maria. Eventually, he proposed marriage to Maria. In so doing, he also told her of the hardships she would have to endure if she were to become the wife of a priest. An Orthodox priest and his *matushka* (title of the wife of a Russian Orthodox priest) must stand as enduring models of connubial faithfulness. They must be pillars of strength and direction for the people in the parish.

Maria was confident that with Valerian at her side, those restrictions he described would not be so hard to bear. She immediately told her mother of Valerian's proposal. Alexandra agreed to the marriage but with the condition that she herself would be able to live with them. Maria and Valerian exchanged their wedding vows in 1892 at the Uspensky Church in Sennaya Square, where Valerian's father Fedot then served as deacon. The bride was sixteen and the groom nineteen.

CHAPTER 2

Birth and Death

Upon completing his studies at the seminary, Valerian, the son of a cleric, was now himself ordained and following the footsteps of his father. He became the priest of a church in the small town of Novorishino near Tsarskoye Selo, otherwise known as the "royal village." This was the vast palace and country home of the Romanov tsars. It lay 15 miles south of St. Petersburg. Five years later, Valerian was given tenancy of the Chapel of St. Nicholas, the wonder-worker at 15, Kosaya Street, in the Municipal District of Vasilievsky Island in St. Petersburg.

This small but important church was situated on the third floor of a large U-shaped brick building which housed, among other things, an orphanage for girls, a school where the orphans studied, and a home for the indigent aged as well as the church. It was built and presented to the monarch by the children of Nicholas and Elena Brusnitsyn, a wealthy couple who accumulated their fortune in the leather trade. Nicholas Brusnitsyn, once a simple tanner, eventually became a partner in the leather-tanning factory where he worked. He accumulated a fortune to such an extent that his family had been able to organize the construction of the enormous U-shaped building with ease. It is recorded that the family spent the huge sum of 1.5 million rubles on its construction. Valerian and his family occupied quarters adjacent to the brick building institution.

It was in this little church on the third floor that the much revered Father John of Kronstadt served, with Valerian as a minor functionary, when the building was consecrated on December 28, 1897. Among those in attendance was the Duke of Oldenburg, brother-in-law of the tsar. Soon after the ceremony, Tsar Nicholas himself visited and expressed his personal gratitude to the donors. For Valerian to serve as a minor functionary at an event attended by the tsar was a glorious honor. He was only twenty-four-year-old and his young Matushka Maria just turned twenty-one. On that occasion, the tsar presented Valerian with a gold watch.

His wife Maria presented him with five children, three sons and two daughters. Valerian's youngest daughter, Valentina, was delivered into the world on January 31, 1902, in the tiny apartment set aside for the chapel priest. She inherited her good looks and a fine bone structure from her father and a twinkle in her eye from her mother. Her birth had been preceded by brothers, Modest and Nicholas, as well as an elder sister, Alexandra (nicknamed Sania). Valentina's birth was followed by that of a younger brother, Kyrill, who died in infancy.

Years later, Valentina recalled that her maternal grandmother, Alexandra, had doted on her and attended to her every whim. In this manner, the little girl developed an uncompromising will when it came to getting her needs met. One day, however, when Valentina's grandmother was out, Valentina threw a temper tantrum, though she doesn't recall why. As she was crying, she heard her mother say to the nanny,

"Let her cry herself out. It won't hurt her a bit—the spoiled little brat!" Valentina was stunned. Never before had she heard herself spoken of in such a harsh manner. Her mother's words bore the traumatic force of a slap in the face, and the strong-willed little girl never forgave her mother for them. This hotly defiant aspect of Valentina's nature was to reveal itself time and again throughout her life. The steel behind her will would enable her to cope with all the difficult situations that she would come to face.

But there was another side to the young Valentina which revealed a nuanced and tender outlook as well. Their home in the brick building on Vasilievsky Island was graced with a beautiful garden. In this garden grew lilacs and rowan trees, and many other flowers of different varieties and colors in summer. In the winter, it was blanketed with snow. Valentina lived in this home until the age of twelve and a half—a first decade of life filled with the bloom of every color. In the spacious garden was also a glass-roofed conservatory that Valentina loved to visit. The gardener of the plants was Jacob, a man in his late 50s, with whom Valentina became fast friends. Throughout the years growing up, it was Valentina's habit when she arrived home from school in the afternoon to go to the conservatory where gentle Jacob talked freely about his botanical philosophy.

"Plants are alive. They feel things just as people do," the sensitive Jacob would tell her. "Now, don't hold that poor creature so tightly, little lady. We don't want to strangle her. Plants are like people . . . They just can't say 'Ouch!' or shed tears like we do. So we must watch out for them."

Valentina's sister, Sania, however, two years her senior, held a different opinion of the place. Whenever Valentina trotted off to the conservatory, Sania would snort, "You and your silly old conservatory!" and shrug dismissively. Their mother, however, merely warned Valentina not to imitate Jacob's Yiddishisms. Either way, Valentina was alone in her fascination for the gentle Jacob and his world of plants.

In the year 1910, Valentina was eight years old. This was also the year that Russia was ravaged by a terrible cholera epidemic. One night during the horrible epidemic, little Valentina was awakened by a commotion in her grandmother's room. Her sister Sania, with whom she shared a room, remained sound asleep, but Valentina, fully awakened, rose from her bed and crept carefully to the door. She peered out. Standing there in her bare feet on the cold night floor, Valentina was transfixed by what she saw: unfamiliar faces running frantically to and fro in the hallway. It was winter, and though a fire burned in the fireplace, Valentina's body shook with a chill and with a fright. Out of the dark night came the voice of her mother screaming for someone to run for a doctor. She also heard her baby brother howling desperately and her grandmother groaning. The telephone rang, and then the front door opened and shut. Suddenly, all was quiet.

Early the next morning, Matushka Maria came in to dress her girls and took them to stay in a hotel off Nevsky Prospect. Later, their father came and admonished them to obey their mother unquestioningly. "We don't want your mother to collapse from exhaustion," he said. "So do exactly as she says."

A few days passed, and then one day, Matushka Maria came back to the hotel, sobbing. In a single night, Maria had lost both her beloved mother, Alexandra, and her precious baby boy to the deadly cholera. The tragedy left her visibly devastated, and Valerian arranged for her to go to Imatra, a Finnish resort, to recuperate. The girls were to take time off from school and accompany her, while the boys remained behind with their father.

The border along Finland, which at that time was a Russian possession, was only an hour away by train from St. Petersburg, and Russian vacationers went there in droves every summer. Imatra, renowned for its waterfall, was a particular favorite. Valentina had been there several times with her family in the summer when the lakes were thick with water lilies and the fields strewn with wild flowers of every imaginable color. In the winter, when the sun came out from behind the clouds, the ice-covered lakes dazzled and the towering conifers mantled in snow glittered like firework sparklers. The roar of the Imatra Falls reverberated through a monochromatic magic wand of varying shades of gray. At night, tucked up in bed, the ceaseless rumbling of the waterfalls kept Valentina awake. When she closed her eyes, the face of her dear, dead babushka Alexandra loomed before her. Her thoughts went back to the time of Alexandra's last rites. The funeral had terrified Valentina, and she had obstinately refused to approach the coffin and give babushka a ritual last kiss. She justified her obstinacy with the reasoning that now her grandmother would forever be alive in her thoughts.

Valentina's obsessive brooding was intensified by news brought by the maid who came to clean their room. It seems that the day before, someone had jumped from the top of the falls. This report and the matter-of-fact tone in which it was delivered horrified Matushka Maria, for she, like most Orthodox followers, held suicide to be a grave sin. The maid hastened to explain, "But, madam, you must understand.

Suicides happen all the time here. People come from all over just to kill themselves. It can't be helped."

Beneath the ice-blue sky, everything in Imatra sparkled and scintillated from the spray thrown up by the cascading water tumbling headlong through the firs and pines to the hotel that glittered like a fairy-tale castle. But death lurked in the shadows of all this beauty. Even the composure of the self-assured Sania crumbled, and a look of alarm settled over her face. With the deaths of her grandmother and brother, Valentina now understood that life was not a path strewn forever with rose petals, extending before her for all eternity, but a brief journey before the terminal blight of death.

That day, after lunch, the two girls and their mother discussed returning to St. Petersburg. Maria had been shaken by what she heard from the maid and was concerned as well about Valerian and the boys. Her daughters agreed with her that the time had come to leave this beautiful but frightening resort.

After only three days in Finland, Maria returned with her daughters to St. Petersburg. She wore only black, pulled her veil down over her face, and began mourning in earnest. For over a month, as was the custom, she attended no social gatherings, participated in no celebrations, and attended repeated Panikhida services for the dead. It seemed likely that she would remain in mourning indefinitely, and the chill emanating from her silence and desperation would continue to weigh upon her family.

Valerian, however, was of the opinion that lengthy mourning periods were unhealthy for children. One day, after supper, as they sipped a cup of tea, he brought up the subject with Maria. Valentina could hear their conversation, which was as follows:

"Growing children shouldn't be made to endure long periods of mourning," he said. "What is important for them is their future. They shouldn't be chained to the past."

Maria listened to her husband in silence.

"What's more, we shouldn't be afraid of death. Jesus gave his life for us sinners, and if we're good, our souls will be saved and we can go to heaven."

"So what is it you want me to do?" Maria asked, wiping away the tears.

"Easter is coming," said Valerian. "Have joy in your heart for the Resurrection of Christ and try to put your sadness behind you. Soon it will be forty days since your mother and our baby died. Forty days is a definite period of prayer for the departed soul. That's long enough for mourning."

"But usually it lasts six months!" Maria persisted. "Some people even wear black and go on mourning for a whole year."

"That's true, but the church doesn't tell us how long a person must mourn. These are just customs that some people choose to observe and others don't."

Maria reluctantly agreed. She would come out of mourning with the arrival of Easter.

CHAPTER 3

Pascha

Pascha is the word for Easter in the Russian Orthodox Church. It was Valentina's favorite holiday, as it was the one time during the entire year when she could stay up all night long. School was also let out for the week following Pascha. However, Pascha came after seven weeks of Great Lent, which was a time of profound solemnity.

The Sunday of Forgiveness came one day before Great Lent started. Valentina did not remember how old she was when she first attended the Sunday of Forgiveness and saw her father, Father Valerian, suddenly prostrate during the service to ask the parish for forgiveness. Gently whispering into her daughter's ear, Matushka Maria urged Valentina to prostrate also. After the service, everyone in the church asked each other for forgiveness. For several minutes, the urgent sounds of "Forgive me for I am a sinner," followed by the customary response "God forgives," dominated the room. The following day, "Pure Monday," the Great Lent began.

Before the Revolution, the Julian calendar, still in use today by the Russian Orthodox and a few other Orthodox churches, was in general use throughout all Russia. Easter in the Russian Orthodox Church falls on the Sunday, following the Jewish Passover, usually later in the calendar year than Easter for Catholic or Protestant churches.

In prerevolutionary days, Russian Orthodoxy was the state religion. By imperial decree, theaters, movie houses, dance halls, and other places of entertainment were shut down during the first and fifth weeks of Great Lent and also during Holy Week. The Orthodox faithful also abstained from certain foods, mainly meat, eggs, and dairy products and did penance for their sins in the Lenten weeks leading up to the day of Pascha.

Preparation for Pascha, however, was not limited to the cumulative seven weeks of abstinence from certain foods and penance for one's sins. As the most important holy day of the year, it was also a busy time of cleaning the house from top to bottom, of laying in stores to grace the Pascha table, and of buying new clothes. And finally, during the week just before Pascha, the glorious smell of Pascha cooking emanates from kitchens throughout Russia. It was by helping in Matushka Maria's kitchen that the young Valentina learned to prepare the many wonderful Pascha dishes.

Traditional Orthodox Easter dishes require a great deal of labor, time, and cooking experience. Traditionally, there was the sweet, cake-like bread called *kulich*, which was baked in tall metal containers. Another tasty dessert, called *pascha* (literally, "Easter"), was shaped like a pyramid and made of pure white, salt-free cheese. Valentina loved to watch as both *pascha* and *kulich* were decorated with sugar candies, spelling the letters XB, the abbreviated form of *Khristos voskrese* (Christ is risen). Even boiled eggs sometimes bore the letters XB painted with food coloring of various hues. It was the duty of Valentina and Sania to color the boiled eggs. After coloring, the eggs were then piled on a plate atop a bed of greens grown especially for this day. The feast was then laid out on an elaborately decorated table. Valentina loved to help her mother decorate the Pascha table with elegance and artistry.

The last week of the long fast from meat, eggs, and dairy products—the week of the Passion—was a solemn time for reflection on the death of Christ by crucifixion. During this time, the faithful, reading passages from the gospel, expressed their grief for the death of the Savior by wearing colors of mourning and of remorse. Special prayers were offered up at churches every day.

On Maundy Thursday, the Thursday of Holy Week, a ceremony was formally observed in which the archbishop of St. Isaac's Cathedral washes the feet of twelve chosen priests. This was an Orthodox tradition based on the passage in the New Testament describing Christ washing the feet of his twelve disciples. One year, Valentina's father, Father Valerian, joined the elect. As the day approached, the humble priest grew increasingly tense. On the appointed day, before setting off for St. Isaac's, he washed his feet several times over lest he should sully the hands of the archbishop.

On Good Friday, church altars and icon stands were draped in black, and the vestments of the clerics were black as well. A wooden sarcophagus was placed in the middle of the church. On top of the sarcophagus was draped a *plashchanitsa*, or shroud, embroidered with an image of Christ after he was taken down from the Cross. Lilies, white lilacs, and white roses were displayed about the sarcophagus.

On the evening of Good Friday, the faithful knelt before the shroud on the sarcophagus, pressing their foreheads to the floor in humility and prayer. After venerating the shroud, they lit candles before it. During the evening service, the lamentation prayers were intoned. Toward the end of the service, the shroud was carried by the priest, and on the shoulders of four lay men chosen for their high esteem in the community. The priest and the men then carried the shroud in a solemn procession in the manner customary of a funeral. This was done once around the church with the faithful following, singing a sacred hymn. After the procession, the shroud was once again returned to the sarcophagus in the center of the church. In the evening of the following day, Holy Saturday, a table was set out near the entrance of the church, and on it parishioners placed the traditional Easter foods *pascha*, dyed eggs, and *kulich* that they made at home. A priest appeared every half hour to bless the foods with a crucifix and holy water. The foods were brought for this very purpose.

At midnight, the Pascha service began. All the candles in the church were extinguished except for a single votive on the altar. The clergy, dressed in white vestments, began singing in a soft and solemn tone, "Thy Resurrection, Oh Christ our Savior, the angels in heaven sing . . ." As the singing grew to a crescendo, the clergy processed out of the darkened altar, followed by the choir and people carrying the icons, banners, lantern, and Cross. The procession then moved out of the church and began to circle the church three times. The congregation joined by following the clergy around the church. After the third time around, the procession stopped in front of the entrance of the church, and the clergy stood in solemn silence as the New Testament told us the women carrying the myrrh and spices so stood. The celebrating priest declared, "Glory to the holy, consubstantial, life-creating, and undivided Trinity." Then the clergy, in unison with each other, sang three times, "Christ is risen from the dead, trampling down death by death, and upon those in the tombs bestowing life!" with the choir repeating the same hymn three times as well. As the clergy and choir sang, the bells pealed with joy and gusto. Then, bells still pealing loudly in the ears of the faithful, the procession turned back into the church where the priest loudly declared to the people, "*Khristos voskrese!*" (Christ is risen!) The people answer back, "*Voistinu voskrese!*" (Truly he is risen!)

In the olden days, before the revolution, the great cathedrals were filled with believers and nonbelievers alike, for this was an annual rite of passage. The bells tolled ceaselessly for three days and three nights while both the faithful and the not-so-faithful patiently waited their turn to pull the ropes. The Royal Doors leading to the altar were left open for the entire week, for it was believed that at Easter, no one was denied entrance to the gates of heaven.

During this Easter time, Valentina would make her way home from church—a candle lit in one hand and a hard-boiled egg grasped in the other—while singing Easter hymns with her sister and brothers. At home, the grandest feast of the year awaited. Father Valerian remained at church, offering up prayers until dawn, but Matushka Maria would return home with the children. Like other people all over Russia, the family sat down to a midnight feast of celebration. On the Pascha day itself, the tradition was to visit family and friends. Everyone was kept on their toes entertaining the constant stream of visitors who had come calling.

Even the children helped to entertain relatives or accompanied the adults when they went to pay their calls. During the Paschal time, it was the practice to exchange greetings *"Khristos voskrese," "Voistinu voskrese"* by kissing each other on the cheeks three times.

The mailmen, guards, and servants would also come to exchange their Paschal greetings with Father Valerian. After they exchanged their greetings and kisses, they would receive from Father Valerian a shot of vodka and an envelope with cash in it. Some of these men had beards. Valentina detested beards and did her best to avoid exchanging kisses with bearded men. She had been told (in jest) that there were cockroaches in beards, and she was certainly influenced by this. Once, a classmate even told her she had seen a mouse dart out of her sleeping father's beard.

As Paschal time drew to a close, the cycle of seasons came around to the "white nights." At their peak—the three weeks from mid-June to early July—the sun never sinks below the horizon in St. Petersburg. Indeed, it was bright enough for Valentina to read a book by the light of the midnight sun. It was at this time of year that Nevsky Prospect filled with promenading young people and families on outings. Lilacs, violets, and Valentina's favorite lilies of the valley were sold at every corner, as they still are today. The town was enfolded in the sweet fragrance of spring flowers.

CHAPTER 4

Tantochka's House

Valentina's great-grandmother, Madame Emilia Myakhnitsova, stepmother of her grandmother Alexandra, was Valentina's oldest living relative. A minor member of the aristocracy, Madame Emilia had once served as a companion to Ekaterina, lady-in-waiting to the Empress Dowager. In the course of her duties to Ekaterina, Emilia would sometimes cross paths with the Royal family. This was an aspect of her job that gave the great lady much cause for pride; and indeed, many times had Valentina heard her great-grandmother proudly exclaim that she had "walked the same corridors as Tsar Alexander III himself." Emilia's livelihood, however, depended on her work with Ekaterina. When Ekaterina married, Emilia found herself demoted into Ekaterina's domestic service. Fortunately for Emilia, she was able to build enough connections of her own to enable her to find a position for her daughter Tatiana that would permit them to live together. This would save Emilia the humiliation of entering the domestic service of Lady Ekaterina.

It was Valentina's linguistically competent mother, Matushka Maria, who dubbed her aunt Tatiana "Tantochka" by joining the German word for aunt with the Russian diminutive suffix. Soon, all of Matushka Maria's children came to know their aunt by that name—regardless of the fact that Tantochka possessed not a drop of German blood! Having lost her position as companion to the lady-in-waiting, Emilia was now forced to live with her daughter, Tatiana or Tantochka, whom she completely dominated. Whenever the girl attempted to act on her own, her mother would not only override her decision but also take her to task for having the temerity to express her volition in the first place. Many times over the years, Tatiana seriously considered breaking with her mother, but the right occasion never came. And in the end, rather than argue with her mother, she followed the path of least resistance and carried out her mother's instructions without a word. Tatiana gradually took to wearing only dowdy and dark-colored clothes and eventually appeared, to those who knew her, to have aged overnight. She became the sort of woman who wouldn't leave the house without first getting her mother's permission, and in time, as the months and years passed, Tantochka came to realize that she was now past marriageable age.

Tantochka's sole diversion in life was casting fortunes with a deck of playing cards, a technique which Valentina quickly learned. But even this was subjected to restriction, and Tantochka was not permitted to indulge in her pastime on days marked on the church calendar as fast days. Seeing the many restrictions in Tantochka's life, Maria begged her grandmother Emilia to give Tantochka more freedom, but her pleas always fell on deaf ears.

The training school where Tantochka worked was established in 1803 for the orphaned children of soldiers and sailors. The houses for teachers, along with classrooms and dormitories, were located on the grounds of the school.

Students of the officer training school ranged from children age six to adolescents of sixteen or seventeen. The older boys were looked after by male teachers and supervisors, while the younger boys were attended to by women teachers such as Tantochka, who also served as a surrogate mother.

Even employment did not offer Tantochka relief from her troubled life with her mother, Emilia. Tantochka was employed as a tutor and mother figure to the young boys enrolled in the officer training school at Gatchina, forty miles southwest of St. Petersburg. Inevitably, however, because of Emilia's obsessive need to control her daughter, she involved herself in her daughter's responsibilities there too.

The school was adjacent to the palace of Crown Prince Tsarevich Paul. Valentina had heard the historical fact directly from Emilia. Paul was the son of Empress Catherine II. Catherine did not favor her son as her successor, however, and instead, treated him with a cool reserve. Paul, in turn, repaid her cold treatment by avoiding St. Petersburg, spent his days at his palace in Gatchina, which ironically was purchased by his mother through imperial fiat for a million and a half rubles and presented to Paul as a gift. Here, he introduced the Prussian style of martial discipline and every day paraded his troops. Catherine scorned his mania for soldiers and doted on her grandson Alexander, whom she groomed as her successor.

The reason for the breach between Paul and his mother lay in the fact that Paul was the child not of Catherine's husband, the Grand Duke Peter, but of her lover Sergei Saltykov. Following her death in 1796, Paul became tsar despite his mother's wishes, but his reign did not last long. He cruelly suppressed serf rebellions and took every opportunity to exercise tsar's autocratic powers. In 1801, he was assassinated in a palace coup in which Crown Prince Alexander played a role.

Valentina often visited Tantochka at Gatchina with her mother and also sometimes her brother, Nicholas. Occasionally, Sania, who as a rule did not enjoy excursions with her brothers and sister, accompanied them. The trip took a little less than an hour by train.

Tantochka had been given living quarters in an apartment building erected in the shadow of the building where she taught, and it was there that she lived with her mother amidst dozens of potted flowers and foliage plants. Their rooms faced the palace, and in the summer, they looked out on luxuriant gardens filled with flowers of every description. Whenever she went to visit Tantochka, Valentina, who was something of a tomboy, would join the younger schoolboys as they climbed the fence separating the school from the palace grounds. On one occasion, the boys scaled the fence entirely and went into the palace gardens and returned with an armload of blossoming lilacs, which they then presented to a beaming Valentina. Valentina completely enjoyed the attention paid to her by the boys; indeed, they were one of the reasons why she liked to visit Tantochka so much. Yet Valentina learned that even the boys felt the weight of her great-grandmother Emilia's presence, at times. One time, noticing a few boys outside playing catch with a ball, Emilia directed Valentina to warn the boys not to break their windows. The boys replied to Valentina, "Don't worry, we're always careful. The old witch would cut our throats if we broke something."

In the apartments where Emilia stayed with her daughter, Emilia kept a huge birdcage in which she housed a pet magpie. Some of the older boys brought her a tree branch, which stood on end within the cage, making it seem as if a tree grew there. In fact, one day, they even discovered that the magpie had built a nest in the makeshift tree. Tantochka did not like the birdcage in the apartment and announced in a tiny voice that their living space was already overcrowded with wall-to-wall potted plants. But, as usual, the protest had not the slightest effect on her despotic mother. Over time, most of the apartment came to be the domain of Emilia and her magpie, while Tantochka's space shrank in size to the equivalent of a train compartment.

As one might expect of a room inhabited by Russian women, the windows were hung with chaste lace curtains, and there were pretty potted geraniums in the window boxes. A holy icon hung in a corner of each room, even in the kitchen. A candle was always burning before each icon. In spite of the tension between mother and daughter, a reverence to God prevailed. Valentina never forgot the warm hominess of Tantochka's apartment and its near-perfect atmosphere of heavenly purity and tranquility.

These visits to Tantochka's home occurred always either during the summer months or during the Paschal holidays and, by custom, involved spending the night. Before going to sleep, the children would pray with their great-grandmother Emilia, and after she had lovingly made the sign of the Cross over each of them, they would serenely drift off to sleep. As Valentina would close her eyes, her great-grandmother would lean over her and, by the light of the votive candle, drop into her mouth a piece of Swiss chocolate. In those instances, half-asleep, Valentina's senses would suffuse with unutterable joy.

On one occasion, however, in this principality of peace deftly reigned over her great-grandmother Emilia, a series of events occurred that ruffled not a few feathers. Items of silverware and jewelry began to disappear one by one. Mother and daughter ransacked the apartment looking for the missing items, but the silver and jewelry were not to be found. Exhausted from their lengthy and unsuccessful searches, the two women sat down and racked their brains, again to no avail whatsoever.

The boys at the officer training school liked to play jokes, but they were well aware that theft was a serious sin. Besides, they were terrified of Madame Myakhnitsova, so there was no reason for Emilia and Tantochka to suspect them. Nor did they suspect the woman who arrived each day to clean. She had been coming to their apartment for years and was like a member of the family.

Who in the world could have come into the dining room? Emilia and Tantochka prayed hard together for restoration of the missing objects, but neither the silver fork, the brooch, the earring, nor the little scissors turned up to solve the riddle.

Then one day, while Valentina chanced to be visiting, the housekeeper let the magpie out while she set about cleaning its cage. Valentina watched as the bird flew about the room and then gasped in amazement as the bird landed, took something shiny in its beak, and flew back with it to the cage. It was great-grandmother's new brooch which she had left out on her dressing table. The magpie immediately went about hiding the brooch in its nest. When Valentina, who had witnessed the avian crime, reached in and shook the tree, out tumbled a silver fork and spoon, along with bits and pieces of jewelry.

The excitement that day was like that of Pascha! Great-grandmother and Tantochka wept for joy and showered kiss after kiss on Valentina, who had so handily cleared up the mystery. Valentina felt proud as a peacock and walked as if on air. Emilia later said to her, "Valya dear, it's not just because the things I'd lost turned up that I was so happy. It was because I knew then that no one had done anything wrong. Think about it." She said, "Wouldn't it have been horrible if it turned out that someone had stolen those things? Wouldn't we have been miserable knowing that there was a thief walking around?"

Valentina's heart filled with love for this old woman, feared by schoolboys and notorious for her unbending manners, who could not even bring herself to condemn the evildoers of the world. Whenever she read in the newspapers of some criminal case taking place, she would unfailingly cross herself and offer a prayer. "Oh, Lord, please protect these poor sinners."

In years to come, Valentina would be forced to leave her homeland and wander from country to country. Wherever she went, however, in her home, a votive always burned before the icons just as a candle burned at Tantochka's place.

CHAPTER 5

Two Brothers

To many people, the notion of a priest's family inevitably brings to mind images of irreproachably well-behaved children. But for the Borotinski family, at least, this was by no means the case, for each of the children possessed a singular nature. They all, in turn, became involved in events that distressed their parents and provided grist for the gossip mill.

Matushka Maria, hardly the spiritual type, had a realistic sense about her. For her, earthly success, fame, honor, and wealth were as important as the salvation of her soul. It was Maria who insisted that the children attend the nonreligious regular school, rather than the parochial school attached to the church. The regular school offered better education.

There was an interval of some two years between the births of each of the surviving four children, so that in 1914, when Valentina, who was the youngest, turned twelve, her brother Modest was already eighteen; Nicholas was sixteen; and her sister Sania, fourteen. They all struggled with troubles they dared not share with their parents.

Modest was now in his final year of high school and was no prodigy; still, his grades gave no cause for complaint. He was blessed with many friends, though he brought only a few to their humble little house by the orphanage. He did not seem to want his friends to know that he was the child of a priest. His parents humored him to the extent they were able, yet he saw them as narrow-minded conservatives who squelched his freedom and gave him inadequate pocket money.

He complained to his friends that his parents refused any discussion of the new liberalist ideas that everyone else was excitedly giving voice to in those days.

Modest was a morose boy who, when he fell into one of his dark moods, would divert himself by shooting his slingshot at a cat that was dear to the superintendent of the orphanage. When that excitement began to pale on him, he then scraped together the necessary parts and made an air gun, which he positioned himself with on the high wall surrounding the garden. Once again the cat was his target. Valentina and Nicholas liked animals and would have acted to save the poor cat from their brother's cruel sport, but they did not know of his action at the time. They could not keep an eye on him all the time, and one day, he shot the cat who barely managed to drag itself back to its master's house.

Their parents knew nothing of Modest's cruelties until an incident occurred, bringing grave concern and deep sadness to the whole family. The teenage son of the deacon at Father Valerian's church was of the same age as Nicholas and had long itched to try out Modest's air gun. Modest was pleased to show off his handiwork, and while giving the boy lessons, Modest accidentally shot the boy in the eye. The boy was rushed to the hospital, but the damage was too great, and he lost sight in one eye.

Father Valerian and Matushka Maria were grief-stricken. They paid all of the boy's medical bills in an attempt to recompense for the accident, but nothing they did could clear the dark cloud of shame that now hung over them. They felt to blame for the accident. Moreover, their sense of personal responsibility was intensified by their son's callous response to their reproaches.

"What's there to say?" Modest retorted. "What has happened has happened. There's no point in brooding over it. After all, it's not as if I took aim at him," Modest continued. "If he hadn't been bumbling around pestering me, the accident wouldn't have happened. It's all his fault. I'm done with apologizing," he said and stomped out of the room. This incident made Valerian and Maria feel that their children were strangers to them. They talked about this often and at length. They placed the blame on the liberalist thinking that was just then taking hold among the young people of the town.

Nicholas, Valentina's senior by four years, was closest to her. Outgoing and a bit mischievous, he was always happy and got along well with his schoolmates. On Sunday afternoons, it was usually Nicholas who brought people into the house. He even had a favorite girl. Whenever young people came, Maria busied herself in the kitchen, but if his friends were girls, she would keep a close watch on them. Often, loud balalaika music and hearty laughter continued until ten o'clock on Sunday nights.

As an alternative to such noisy parties, the children were sometimes taken to the movies, the opera, or the ballet. It was Maria's conviction that the theater was essential to the children's education.

The Borotinski children all learned to play the piano, but like most children, after reaching a certain level of proficiency, progress came to a halt. Only Sania continued with the piano lessons longer than her siblings. Valentina's brother,

Nicholas, showed great promise as an artist and an actor. It was Maria who first recognized his artistic ability and, as a high school student, sent him to evening classes at a private art academy. Nicholas's sketchbook impressed his teachers, who said his portraits showed genuine talent. In the theater, his performance in a comedy staged with other young actors earned favorable mention in critical reviews. But as the saying goes, "Man proposes, God disposes," nothing at all came of these promising talents.

At the orphanage where Father Valerian served, there was a Finnish gate guard named Spirka. Nicholas, who had gained a taste for vodka, began visiting Spirka in his little room to share a bottle, instead of taking the crowded train to his evening art class. For a young man eager to live dangerously, the room was a far more attractive place than the art school. One day, Maria, planning to send her son to the prestigious St. Petersburg Art Academy after he finished high school, stopped at the school to confer with his teachers. She learned that Nicholas had for some time been absent from school. Maria grilled the boy until he confessed and elicited that he had been drinking with Spirka. Father Valerian realized that Spirka would lose his job if he were reported to his superiors, so he chose to remain silent. He punished Nicholas, however, by requiring him to ask permission before going out and further warning him that if he ever went to visit Spirka again, his friend would lose his job. To her dismay, Maria also found sausages and cheese in Nicholas's room during Lent. That, plus his drinking convinced Maria that Nicholas did not believe in God and ignored Lent.

CHAPTER 6

A Sister

Sania, whose real name was Alexandra, was two years older than Valentina and displayed behavior that was no less inappropriate for the child of a priest than had her brothers. At any school, at any time, bullying is a problem, and it was in such victimizing behavior that Sania became involved.

One day, Valentina arrived home in a state of great agitation. Before entering the room she shared with her sister, she stuck her head into Nicholas's room and asked if she could come in. Taking note of her anxiety, Nicholas said, "Sure. Come in."

Valentina entered and quietly closed the door, and then she began, in hushed tones, to tell Nicholas what was bothering her.

"I can't make any sense of it."

"Of what?"

"Well, in school today, Sania made a point of being really nice to me. When I met her in the hallway, she suddenly took me by the hand. A tall girl, one of Sania's classmates, was with her, and Sania introduced me to her as 'my sister whom I dearly love.' She has never said she loved me before, so it made me really happy."

Valentina paused to wipe away a tear.

"So why are you sad?"

"Well, I was so happy I thought I'd walk home from school with her today. We've never done that, you know. As usual, Sania was late, but I waited. Then when she finally came, she said, 'Are you some kind of idiot or something? You really think I love you? Wise up!'"

Nicholas thought for a moment. "Sania may have a good head," he said, "but she's coldhearted, and so she takes pleasure in teasing you. It's like when Modest tortured the cat. Don't let her get to you. Modest doesn't treat me so well either, you know."

The two promised not to speak to their parents about what had happened, and Valentina, now certain she could confide in her brother, reported to Nicholas what she had heard at school about Sania's bullying.

Although Sania was not the top of her class, she was highly competitive and constantly itched to win the gold medal, an award given to the student with the best academic record. To this end, she often complained that her mathematics teacher, who taught the only subject that gave her trouble, was playing favorites to her disadvantage.

Sania's classmates, wary of her acid tongue and barbed criticisms, largely steered clear of her. However, there was one student, Yulia, in whom Sania took particular delight in bullying. Yulia was a tall, lethargic, rail-thin girl, with pasty skin and hair pulled back tightly into a bun. She was quiet and seldom talked to other students. Yulia never once complained to her teachers about the girls who were bullying her. One of the girls spread a rumor that Yulia had adopted a folk remedy for hair loss by putting a potato in her bun. This sparked amusement among the cruel girls, and some of them approached her to ask if the rumor was true. They were amused when Yulia's face turned red with embarrassment. Sania was among this band of baiters, though the leader was a Swedish girl, Mura Tavasherna, who always wore a sardonic smile. Mura, too, was tall, if a bit plain, and like Sania, she possessed a quick wit and a glib tongue. Anyone so bold as to laugh at her soon had the tables turned on them. When it came to teasing the introverted and clumsy, Mura was masterful and merciless.

One day, Sania came home from school and reported to her mother that she and Mura had been invited to a birthday party at Yulia's house. Maria, who had for some time been troubled by Sania's attitude toward Yulia, thought things over for a moment and then replied, "Sania, I think you should go to the party. No doubt Yulia's parents have invited you so that you'll stop teasing their daughter. They probably thought that if you and your friend visit their home, you'll get to know her better and be nice to her. You may discover that Yulia is much brighter than you give her credit for. I'll get a present ready for you to take."

Sania had imagined that her mother would not want her to go. She began to whine. "But Yulia's really dumb! She's terrible at math!"

"You're not that much better at mathematics, I should think," Maria replied. "I went to see your teacher today. And he told me that if you really want to win the gold medal, then I should get somebody to tutor you in math at home."

Sania bit her lip. She regretted having told her mother about the invitation. If she hadn't mentioned it, she could have turned the invitation down on her own. *How depressing it is*, she thought, *to have to go to the birthday party of a classmate who deserved nothing but ridicule and contempt!* The next day at school, Sania told Mura what her mother had said and was surprised to learn that Mura's father, who was a hard-nosed businessman, had given her a similar reply.

The birthday party was on Sunday afternoon. As they had agreed upon, Sania met Mura near Yulia's house so that the two could arrive together. Sania, who had been thinking of how best to keep the upper hand, discussed with Mura ways to make the party a cold and joyless event. They wanted it to be apparent to all that they had come to the party simply to observe social propriety.

They were in for a surprise. Sania and Mura rang the bell at the entrance, but no one came to the door. They could hear the patter of running feet and shouting inside the house. Apparently, something entirely unforeseen was happening. The two looked at each other and wondered aloud whether they should wait for the door to open or simply go home. Just then, the door opened, and a young maid appeared. She looked deathly pale as she told them that Ms. Yulia had suddenly fallen ill and that a doctor had been sent for. The maid told that Yulia's mother sent her apologies to the girls at the door.

The next day, the teacher gathered everyone together to report that the day before, on her sixteenth birthday, Yulia had passed away. She explained to the astonished students that Yulia had been born with heart trouble and often had to stay home from school because of it. Recently, however, Yulia had been particularly depressed over her health, and so her parents came up with the plan of inviting all of Yulia's classmates to a grand birthday celebration. But the preparations and the excitement of what should have been a wonderful party was too great a burden for her poor heart to bear. Yulia had a heart attack when the first guests arrived and had died almost immediately.

When Sania reported Yulia's death to her mother, it was clear she felt the prick of conscience. She and Mura had been the first guests to arrive.

As she listened to her daughter's account, she had asked herself whether Sania and Mura alone were to blame or whether she, as a parent, held some measure of responsibility for the girl's death. As she continued to weigh the matter in her mind, she also wondered if the teacher was also to blame. *Yulia had a bad heart. Shouldn't the girl's teacher have anticipated the worst and informed her classmates of Yulia's health?* Maria's thoughts continued, *Had Yulia been in anguish worrying over how she should receive those of her classmates who disliked her?* Surely Yulia agonized over what those two mean-spirited girls might do and what she should say in response.

Maria felt a deep compassion for Yulia's mother. What if her own daughter had been in Yulia's position? Perhaps she had been wrong to insist that Sania attend the party.

Sania, too, was deeply troubled. No one at home spoke of the tragedy, but Valentina learned from the talk at school some additional lurid details, unknown to the rest of the family, details of her sister's role in Yulia's suffering. It seems it was Sania, who had relentlessly bullied Yulia and made her the laughingstock of the whole school. Valentina felt sorry for Yulia and was both disgusted and ashamed whenever she heard the gossip detailing the teasing inflicted on Yulia and other weaker girls by Sania and Mura.

Sania expected herself to receiving a severe scolding from her parents. Valerian, however, said nothing. Instead, he gazed on his daughter with silent eyes of love and deep compassion.

He decided the best way to make Sania feel remorse was for him not to respond overtly.

"There's only one thing I want you to tell Sania to do," he said to Maria. "When Sania next goes to confession with her godfather, I want her to tell him what she has done."

In the Russian Orthodox Church, a godfather or a godmother was chosen at the time of baptism to serve as a child's spiritual mentor. Sania's godfather was an aged monk at the Alexander Nevsky Monastery in St. Petersburg. In the eyes of the world, therefore, the incident of Sania's bullying thus came to an end, and she was left to plumb the depths of her remorse alone and at length under the direction of her spiritual mentor.

In spite of these problems, though, Sania remained Matushka Maria's favorite daughter. Although she did her best to give the best education to both girls, only Sania excelled in all her studies, including piano and French lessons. Valentina, on the other hand, was a reasonably good student, but she was not as ambitious as her sister, who thought always about winning the gold medal in her class. Valentina was simply not interested in being the top of the class, and she could not beat Sania in academics. Maria came to the conclusion that it would be best if Valentina learned more practical skills such as cooking, housekeeping, sewing, and embroidery. Her two brothers laughed at this, saying that Valentina was the Cinderella of the house. Offended by the implications of this remark, Matushka and Sania complained to Father Valerian. He responded, "What is wrong with being Cinderella? She was surely a good girl." Father Valerian had simply missed the point that if Valentina was called Cinderella, then Matushka and Sania would be called the cruel stepmother and the ugly stepsister.

CHAPTER 7

Calf-Love

Since the death of her younger brother who died in infancy, Valentina had been brought up as the baby of the family and proved to have a personality no less singular than her sister and two brothers. Although headstrong and doggedly tenacious, she had another more endearing side in which she came across as extremely credulous and excruciatingly naive. Her first, unrequited, excursion in the name of love makes abundantly clear the depths of her naïveté.

In the spring of her twelfth year, Valentina was growing into a beautiful young girl with dark blonde hair and peaches-and-cream complexion. As do many girls her age, she dreamed of a handsome knight in shining armor. Although she had no contact with her brother Nicholas's friends outside her house, they often came on visits, so she had opportunities to meet young men. None of them, however, approached her standards.

Around this time, Valentina became friends with a classmate, Seraphima, who soon became Valentina's closest friend. Maria, in turn, decided that Seraphima was a proper young lady and permitted Valentina to visit her house and to receive visits from Seraphima in return. Seraphima, however, came from a very different sector of society than that in which Valentina was raised.

In Valentina's conservative family, the supervision and discipline of her education-minded mother were strict, and the children's freedom was seriously monitored. Not only were they required to get permission before going out of the house, but they also had to report where they were going and how long they would be gone. Even her elder brothers had not, until recently, been allowed to go out unless accompanied by a servant. Seraphima, on the other hand, grew up in an emancipated family of artists.

Seraphima's businessman father was a widower and was rarely at home. Seraphima's brother was a musician engaged in the training of young opera singers, one of whom was his fiancée. She lived in the house and managed household affairs. Seraphima's elder sister was a university student who was studying drama, and so it happened that people with connections to the theater, including actors, actresses, and singers, were always coming and going in Seraphima's house. Although still only a young age, in the absence of her mother, Seraphima was free to do as she wished.

Maria was unaware of these details of domestic life at Seraphima's home and knew only that Seraphima belonged to a family of artists. She had once met Seraphima's sister, who was a woman of entrancing beauty. Having had no previous contact with artists and knowing nothing of their lifestyle, Maria was unconcerned about what went on at Seraphima's.

When Valentina called on her, Seraphima would describe the splendid parties that had been held at her house, the plots or entertaining scenes from plays and operas which she went to see every week, or anecdotes about the great performing artists. Valentina listened closely to these stories, deeply attracted by Seraphima's way of life, which was so utterly different from her own and which exuded the allure of art. Sometimes, when she spoke to Seraphima on the telephone, Valentina would hear background voices raised in songs or the bubbling laughter of actors and singers gathered in the living room. Seraphima would joke that in order to hear anything at all on the phone she had to wear a big cushion over her head. At that time, there were no telephones in the houses of ordinary people in St. Petersburg, but their use had spread quite widely among people in prominent positions and among the bourgeoisie.

One day, having been invited to Seraphima's home, Valentina got her mother's permission and went out. It was early afternoon on a Saturday, the day when her father conducted vespers, and Maria warned her to get back in time to go. Vespers on Saturday was at 6:00 p.m.

When she arrived at Seraphima's place, Valentina found her alone and unhappy. Everyone had gone to a concert while Seraphima stayed behind. Seraphima showed none of her customary liveliness and seemed dispirited, even troubled.

"Something's happened?" Valentina asked.

Seraphima nodded, and one by one, she revealed a few of her secrets.

Her brother's fiancée, whom she hated, had taken charge of the whole household. She supervised everything, even domestic spending. When Seraphima asked for money to buy a new pair of socks or gloves, the fiancée would always turn her down. Seraphima's revelations now touched on graver matters.

Seraphima's father was a member of the council at a certain church and was entrusted with the management of the church's finances and collection of donations from the congregation. One Sunday, when he was busy with other matters, he asked Seraphima and another parishioner to take up the collection for him. On the way to the church office, collection plate in hand, Seraphima began to think about the socks and things that she wasn't able to buy and decided to pocket a portion of the money. As she confessed her crime to her dearest friend, she was overwhelmed with regret for what she had done and began to cry.

Valentina was horror-struck by the enormity of her friend's act. *My God! She stole from the collection plate!*

Seeing the fear and revulsion register on Valentina's face, Seraphima instantly regretted confiding in her and, jumping to her feet, went to wash away her tears. When she returned, they sat in uneasy silence, each thinking thoughts she dared not share with the other.

Then the doorbell rang, and Seraphima rose to answer it. Through the door came a handsome student; judging by the stand-up collar and gold uniform buttons, the young man was a student at a prestigious school. He had dark eyes, black hair, and an unusual look of nobility that Valentina was not accustomed to seeing. Seraphima introduced the boy as Volodya, a distant cousin, who was taking singing lessons from Seraphima's brother.

Volodya, whose abrupt appearance had saved the two girls from their awkward silence, made them laugh with his funny stories about school life, and soon the unpleasantness vanished from Valentina's mind. For a while, she even forgot about vespers. Then, suddenly realizing that it was fast approaching six, she excused herself and set out for home with Volodya, who had gallantly offered to escort her. As Valentina's house was within walking distance, the two strode the distance shoulder-to-shoulder and parted with warm good-byes.

The two girls were spared from the uncomfortable moment, but the quality of the friendship afterward was undoubtedly changed. Seraphima was no longer as frank as she had once been with Valentina, and, indeed, never again did she mention her animosity toward her brother's fiancée, much less the stolen money from the collection plate.

Valentina's name day, the feast of the Martyr Valentina on February 23, was approaching. In Russia, it was the practice to celebrate name days in grander style than birthdays. Not only was a special meal prepared and a cake baked, but presents and cards were given to friends and family.

When they met at school on Valentina's name day, Seraphima offered her congratulations and pressed Valentina's hands a white envelope. She said it was from Volodya. Seraphima explained that as he hadn't known Valentina's address, he had sent it through her. Valentina was beside herself with astonishment. Trying her best to control the pounding in her breast, she opened the envelope and took out a pretty card with a heart drawn on it and in one corner, the following message of two or three lines:

"Congratulations on your name day. Have you been well? How is school?"

This was the first letter that Valentina had ever received from a boy. Her surprise and great joy were obvious to Seraphima. Four or five days later, Seraphima approached her again. "The next time Volodya came for his singing lesson, he asked me if you had reacted to the card." Then, studying Valentina's face closely, she went on, "Volodya seems to like you. I think he wants you to answer."

Valentina had no idea what to write. After all, she'd never sent a message to a boy before, not to mention a boy as fine as Volodya. But Seraphima kept on urging her to write.

"Volodya is very sad because he hasn't received a letter. He keeps pestering me for news of you."

Seraphima confessed to having a warm spot herself for the handsome Volodya. She said that it irked her that he showed no interest in her. Still, because she liked him, she wanted for him to have what he desired and so was happy to act as go-between. Valentina felt deeply moved by all this but, at the same time, strangely alone. Was there no one to whom she could talk to about all this? Her family members were the last people in the world in whom she could confide.

Every time Valentina and Seraphima met, Seraphima would urge her to write just a few lines to poor besotted Volodya, and finally, in a trembling hand, Valentina wrote a reply.

They began to exchange love letters on a regular basis. Not only did they write tirelessly of life and love, of music and of literature, but they even exchanged their favorite poems. Seraphima assumed the role of letter carrier. Valentina sometimes wondered aloud why Seraphima didn't arrange a meeting with him at her house, but there always seemed to be a credible reason why it wasn't possible. Volodya was studying for his end-of-term examinations, or Volodya always came on Saturday evenings when Valentina was attending vespers.

Little by little, spring drew nigh, and soon it was upon them. Buds opened in parks and gardens, and lilies of the valley, violets, and lilacs went on sale at stalls, lining the great avenues.

One day, when Valentina had finished studying in the library for her year-end exams, she came upon a wagon just outside the school gates filled with flowers. Counting out the few pennies left over from her carfare, she bought a little posy of violets and set out for home. As she crossed bridge after bridge over the canals, she bent her thoughts toward Volodya and the content of his most recent letter.

Suddenly, there he came, striding toward her. Volodya seemed to be in a hurry and apparently had not yet caught sight of her. The distance between them narrowed, and then, with a look of surprise, he stopped in front of her. "Oh, I'm sorry. I didn't recognize you. Why, yes, it was at Seraphima's house that we met, wasn't it?"

For a moment, she couldn't believe her ears. *After all those letters we exchanged, he doesn't recognize me?*

Volodya seemed ill at ease as he rattled on about school and his family and their plans to visit Moscow in summer.

"Volodya!" she said, almost shouting. "You never even mentioned Moscow in your last letter!" It was obvious that he had no idea what she was talking about.

"My last letter, you say?"

Valentina nodded with a look of deepening perplexity.

"Letter? I don't recall ever writing you a letter. What in the world are you talking about?"

Valentina could carry the conversation no further.

She had no recollection of how she got home. The shock kept her out of school for several days. Thinking up an excuse to stay at home, she told her mother that she had a splitting headache and could not study. She did not want to see

Seraphima or any of her other classmates. But the year-end exams could not be ignored. She could not just stop going to school.

When at last she showed her face at school, she was met by that day's class monitor, Anastasia, a girl of congenitally weak constitution who often missed school. Anastasia wore a perpetual look of melancholy and, perhaps because she was a few years older than her classmates, tended to speak with an earnest solemnity.

"What an idiot you are! Everyone but you knew what Seraphima was up to. Seraphima even got people to write letters in the boy's name. Didn't you notice the different hands?"

Valentina had, in fact, thought it odd that each of her letters from Volodya seemed to be written in a different hand. Once she had even asked Seraphima, who replied, "Oh, really? I guess Volodya must have been in a hurry. Famous novelists and poets are like that too, you know. And they sometimes have the most terrible handwriting."

So self-assured was Seraphima's response that Valentina felt ashamed to have mentioned it.

At last Valentina understood why almost no one in her class trusted the oh-so-cunning Seraphima. Anastasia offered Valentina encouragement and advised her to be wiser in her choice of friends, but Valentina was too devastated to reply. She never forgot what Seraphima had done to her, but neither did she ever learn from the experience. This naïveté was to plague Valentina all her life. At the same time, however, it was an indication of the constancy and depth of her feelings.

CHAPTER 8

Journey to Crimea

It was time once again for year-end exams, but this year, Sania and Valentina were spurred on to persevere by the prospect of spending the summer together in sunny Crimea. For some weeks, Matushka Maria had been making plans with her friend, Christina Ivanovna, wife of the chapel's cantor, regarding this trip. They planned to travel with two young girls together to the Crimean Peninsula. Maria was well aware of its scenic beauty, but she also wanted her children to appreciate the region as representing the southernmost reaches of the vast territories that constituted Imperial Russia. Maria, who believed that travel was the best education a child could have, put together a carefully considered itinerary each summer. Two years earlier, she had taken her daughters to Kiev in Ukraine, the mother of all Russian principalities.

By 1914, the domestic political situation had grown increasingly tense, and as the day of their departure for the Crimea drew near, there were even rumors of approaching war. But Maria decided that, at least for the duration of the summer, the world would remain intact, and she went ahead with her plans to journey with her two daughters. Modest and Nicholas would remain behind in St. Petersburg with their father. If the boys went along, it would mean renting an extra room at considerable added expense. At any rate, they had reached the age when traveling with one's parents was no longer an exciting prospect for them.

Finally, the day of their departure arrived. It was a two-and-a-half-day journey by train from St. Petersburg to Crimea. Valentina's eyes were alight with excitement as the train chugged its way past emerald-green meadows, dark forests, great rivers, and broad lakes. Then the fertile black-earth fields of Ukraine and a succession of whitewashed farmhouses surrounded by blossoming fruit trees — peaches, plums, and apricots — came into sight, as she later recalled.

Finally, she saw Rocky Mountains, the green fields, and the deep-blue waters of the Black Sea. At Sudak, the resort in Crimea where they had arranged to stay, there were no hotels. Lodgings for tourists consisted of one- or two-story cottages. Maria and the girls settled into a large room with three beds in a two-story cottage situated on a slope overlooking the sea. Their traveling companion, Christina Ivanovna, took a smaller room in the same cottage.

In stark contrast to the dark-gray sea and ink-washed sky of their native Baltic, the Black Sea was an entrancing cerulean blue beneath azure skies. Every day, they swam in the waters or walked in the foothills of the lofty mountains surrounding Sudak. Because of the area's fertile soil and warm climate, grapes grew in abundance, and there were also peaches, apricots, plums, strawberries, and a number of other fruits. The gardens that rimmed the blue sea blazed with flowers of every imaginable color, mostly crimson rose bushes set against a background of whitewashed cottages. As far as Valentina was concerned, Crimea was paradise on earth. Her joy was dimmed only by the single fact that no sooner had they arrived, Maria, the resourceful educationist, had come up with a native French speaker to tutor her daughters in French. Nevertheless, the free and easy days of their holiday seemed to pass by ever so slowly, like one long, lazy summer afternoon's dream.

One day, a telegram came from Father Valerian. Maria was not able to understand its contents until several more had arrived. Finally, Valerian's hoped-for advancement in the church hierarchy had come through. He had been appointed priest of the parish surrounding Uspensky Church in the heart of St. Petersburg where his father Fedot had been first a reader and later a deacon. As a consequence, the Borotinski family soon moved into the rectory in a corner of the church precincts. Uspensky Church was known far and wide as the church with the largest and wealthiest congregation in all of St. Petersburg.

What splendid news! Valentina had craved a room of her own, and since there were seven rooms in the new house, there would be no need for her to double up with Sania. Valerian's dream had come true. Valentina knew but let it be noted that in order to become parish priest of a large church in the capital city, it was not enough simply to have graduated from a seminary. A far deeper knowledge of theology was required. She also knew that for a number of years, Father Valerian had continued his studies at St. Petersburg Theological Academy, and now his unrelenting efforts had borne fruit.

Valentina's mother, Maria, had helped him with his success. As a young girl attending the local girls' school in the town of Perm in the northern Ural Mountains, Maria had studied French, German, Latin, and other languages and had been able to help her husband fulfill some of his scholastic requirements.

That Father Valerian should become the priest of such a great church was Maria's wish as well. If Valerian presided over a church with a congregation of prosperous merchants, Maria reasoned, they could expect increased earnings, enabling them to give their children a better education.

As the remaining days of their vacation dwindled, Maria, the pedagogue, went about arranging berths on a boat that called at ports around the perimeter of the Black Sea. She especially wanted her daughters to see Sevastopol, the homeport of Russia's Black Sea Fleet.

One morning, as Valentina was returning from her daily visit to the fruit market with a basket of grapes and peaches, she was met by a group of people desperately trying to make themselves heard above a clamor of voices. As she approached, she saw that there were some university students in the hallway anxiously taking turns reading a newspaper. Wondering what had happened, Valentina drew near. A young female student shouted to her, "Hurry and tell your mother war's been declared!"

Valentina was at a loss for what to think. If the news of war were true, it meant that the pleasant vacation and Valerian's promotion had come to a premature end. Gathering up her courage, she asked, "Who with?"

"Germany . . . and probably Turkey!" yelled the student. "Russia's near them both. It could be bad. Turkey is on the other side of the Black Sea, of course. If they should . . ."

Valentina had heard enough and raced off to tell her mother, who was equally stunned by the news.

"How can it be? How could it happen without some warning?"

Maria then realized that since coming to Crimea, she hadn't read the newspapers and few people had discussed current events. Calming herself, Maria ran off to ask the students for details on the pending war. She learned that on the previous day, July 20, 1914, Nicholas II had signed a declaration of war on Germany at the Winter Palace. At that moment, Germany's ally, Turkey, began sending forces into Crimea. The fact that the Turkish fleet could attack Crimea at will caused the vacationers to panic. The students told her that on June 28, prior to these events, Archduke Francis Ferdinand and his wife Sophie had been assassinated while on a state visit to Sarajevo by Gavrilo Princip, a nineteen-year-old Bosnian Serb.

This incident had prompted Austria-Hungary to declare war on Serbia. Russia announced its readiness to stand by Serbia's side, and France declared its support for Russia. Germany, whose aim had been imperialist expansion, announced that it would fight on the side of Austria-Hungary. Between these irreconcilably opposed alliances of nations, there would soon be waged a war so extensive that it was known even in its time as The Great War.

Maria was desperate to get back safely to St. Petersburg with the girls beneath her protective wings. Many of her fellow vacationers were in hysterics. The schedule for trains leaving Crimea was in disarray. Tickets for sleeping berths were all but impossible to obtain.

Forcing herself to think logically, Maria came to the conclusion that the worst possible circumstance would be for the family to get separated. She was also worried that Modest, her eldest son, might at any moment be conscripted.

After speaking first with the students and then with both the landlady and her friend, Christina Ivanovna, and also with as many local people as possible, Maria decided to take the first train leaving Crimea and distance themselves from the threat the resort area would likely face. Everyone hurriedly gathered their luggage and joined the crowd of people making their way toward the already packed trains. They could not obtain tickets for sleeping berths only for ordinary seats, yet they felt grateful for any tickets.

This sort of crisis was a first-time experience for Valentina, and she was fascinated by the extreme excitement, even by the outright panic that it evoked in people. Both Maria and Christina Ivanovna were rigid with apprehension, but Valentina and Sania quickly made friends with the other children in the train. Together, they prattled on gaily about decisions their parents had taken whose dire consequences they could barely imagine. The train, with its burden of passengers, young and old, raced on through the dark night toward St. Petersburg.

CHAPTER 9

Petrograd

Military trains were given priority, and the passenger train carrying Valentina and the others was stopped time and time again before finally arriving at St. Petersburg's Moscow Station. Matushka Maria called on the station telephone for someone to come and get them. As it happened, Father Valerian wasn't at home, but Modest and Nicholas came and helped Maria with the luggage. The usually voluble Nicholas said little and was irritable, while Modest, normally reticent, chattered on at length. Maria busied herself assigning responsibility for the various pieces of luggage. Sania looked tired and was in an evil mood. Valentina alone seemed to sense that her brothers were keeping something from them. When they arrived at home, Valerian was waiting for them, but it was late, and they were all exhausted, so they went to bed.

The next morning at breakfast, Father Valerian looked solemn. He announced to the assembled family, "As you know, Russia and its ally France have taken on both Germany and Austria-Hungary in war. Of course, we too must do our part along with the many families of our congregation. We mustn't despair. It's not the end of the world. The war will soon be over."

Satisfied that he had adequately prefaced the remarks that were to follow, he straightened himself and curtly announced, "Modest has been drafted."

Modest himself was still in bed. Nicholas stared in silence at the plate in front of him, and Valentina wondered if everyone whose brother or son had received a draft notice had reacted with this same mixture of sadness and trepidation.

When he came down to breakfast, even Modest was confused as to how he should feel. The draft notice had made his existence important, and he basked in a glow of romantic heroism. However, there lurked in the background the thought that a battlefield might not be a very pleasant place to find himself in.

Modest, then a student at Putilov Technological University in St. Petersburg, had been told that he would be sent to officers' training school before being conveyed to the front to fight for the glory of the tsar against the Germans, the Austrians, or the Turks.

The news of Modest's conscription made it impossible to take joy in Valerian's promotion or the move to their new home. Valentina did feel happy, however, that at least for the time being, she would have a measure of privacy. Valentina's first room had formerly been the sewing room. It was small and cozy and had wallpaper with pink flowers on it. A big window, from which you could look down over the city, was framed in white lace curtains. There was a wardrobe, a chest of drawers, and a little chair and table. In one corner of the room, there was a bed that was just the right size for a teenage girl. The rectory at 40, Sadovaya Street, which shared a big back garden with the church, was comfortable and roomy. Jacob, the gardener, however, was no longer with them, nor was the nursemaid who had once been so sweet to Valentina. She had a family of her own now.

In her stead, Maria hired a young Polish housekeeper with modern notions. Maria also arranged with a woman, whose husband, for business reasons, was temporarily residing in France to serve as a live-in French tutor for her daughters. The house was huge, and Maria arranged for two of her husband's nieces, whose mother had passed away, to stay with her family until they had mastered a skill and could support themselves when they came of age.

For some time before the trip to Crimea, Valentina had become aware that on occasion, her parents discussed domestic political issues or Russia's foreign policy, but she did not share their interest in the issues. They attributed the poor diplomatic relations between Russia and Germany to the expansionist pressures exerted by Germany and Austria on the southern Slavic states. But Valentina did not connect this knowledge with a visceral awareness of the mayhem that war casually inflicts on all who stray into its path. After all, she was still a child, and it tested the limits of her imagination even to think that if there were a war, then somewhere many soldiers would get killed. Also she expected that she would not be able to travel everywhere on the train. On August 31, 1914, the capital city's Germanic name, St. Petersburg, changed to the Slavic Petrograd.

It seemed to Valentina that conversations at the new rectory between her parents and their friends and acquaintances were turning to subjects of a darker nature. Ugly gossip about Tsar Nicholas II and his consort Alexandra had began to circulate probably because the empress, who was of German extraction, was unpopular with the Russian people. Even as he was being crowned tsar of all Russia on May 26, 1896, events had unfolded that encouraged the rumors.

At the culminating moment of the tsar's coronation, his necklace of gems fell from his shoulder and loudly crashed to the floor. His retinue feared that his subjects might take this as an ill omen. They instructed those who had been close enough to hear the crash not to breathe a word of it to anyone.

The following day, there was a reception in Khodynka Square to honor the new tsar and tsarina. Khodynka Square was the parade ground of the Moscow Garrison, and everywhere there were ditches and moats. Although there was no other place where tens of thousands of people could gather, it was nevertheless not the safest site available.

It had been announced that a commemoration souvenir would be given away, and many people stood in line overnight. By dawn, a crowd of about 500,000 awaited the arrival of the tsar. The good and simple people who gathered on the parade ground wanted only to catch a glimpse of the tsar and tsarina and to bless them. Someone shouted that the free beer was running out, and it was first come, first served. Word spread in a flash, and a surge of people descended on the square. The troop of guards, which was there to protect the people, was shoved aside, and a number of celebrators stumbled into one or another of the excavations or were crushed underfoot. When the police and the Cossack horsemen arrived on the scene, the square looked like the aftermath of a battle. Many people believed that the incident was a portent of evil things to come during the reign of the new tsar.

On the night of this tragedy, in which more than two thousand people died and many more were hurt, a ball had been planned at the French Embassy for the tsar and tsarina. When she learned of the tragedy that had befallen her people, the Dowager Empress Maria Fyodrovna issued a command to cancel the ball and all other festivities immediately. However, the new emperor and empress felt obliged to recognize by their presence the painstaking efforts that had been made to bring from France the elegant silverware, porcelain, and thousands of roses, and they went ahead with the grand ball. Inevitably, this rankled with their subjects.

The dropped jewels during the coronation and the catastrophic public celebration the following day were merely the opening scenes of a relentless five-act tragedy to come. Later, Russia's stunning defeat, both on land and at sea, in their war with Japan (1904-05) weakened the Russian people's confidence in their tsar. Bloody Sunday (1905), which primed the pump for the Revolution, and Crown Prince Alexei's affliction with hemophilia cast a pall over all Russia. But most ominous of all was the tsar's inability to rally either the affection or the respect of his people. The emperor dearly loved his German consort, but she was as unpopular with aristocracy and commoners alike. She spoke Russian poorly; she was sensitive to the point of irritability, and she suffered from spells of depression. The birth of an heir with hemophilia further lowered her popularity. But very few people knew of Alexei's hemophilia.

The empress had become a devoted adherent of the Russian Orthodox Church and, as is sometimes the case with converts to the faith, was attracted to its mystical tradition. She was readily taken in by unscrupulous politicians and religious charlatans. Among the latter was Rasputin, a mystic who gained nationwide notoriety for his hypnotic eyes and the cruel deceptions he worked on her and the tsar through manipulating their fears for their hemophiliac son, on whom they both doted.

From 1914 to 1916, Rasputin lived at 66, Gorokhovaya Street, around the block and across the Fontanka Canal — from the Borotinski's new residence. Neighbors would see him walking by, and he was often the subject of discussion at Father Valerian's rectory. Once Valentina and her mother had passed him in the street when out for a walk. True to his reputation, his piercing gaze had seemed to dart out at them. Valentina recalled being deeply disturbed by the impression he made on her.

According to what Valentina heard from her parents, Rasputin was a member of the heretical Khlysty sect, whose adherents believed that it was necessary to sin in order to experience repentance. He was neither a priest in the Russian Orthodox Church nor one of its monks, and so he did not have any formal standing in the Orthodox Church. Nevertheless, he referred to himself as the "Divine Cleric" and announced that he had been sent by God to save Holy Russia. People in the neighborhood could testify to the dissolute life he led and the merrymaking at nightly parties, attended by a strange assortment of characters including aristocratic ladies and common streetwalkers.

Members of the nobility submitted reports of Rasputin's excesses the emperor and empress who, in 1911, banned him from their court. The empress, however, arranged for his return visit within months. And thereafter, Tsar Nicholas yielded to her every wish regarding Rasputin. From 1915, the tsar went to the front to take direct command of his troops, leaving the government in the hands of his consort Alexandra and her principal advisor, Rasputin.

In the eyes of the common people, Nicholas was a totally ineffectual monarch who had abandoned them to the autocratic whim of his German consort and her diabolic Rasputin.

CHAPTER 10

Ideologues Flock Home

War or no war, the new school year began in September as it always did. Though the students were a year closer to graduation, they still had the same homeroom teacher. It seemed to Valentina that during school hours, she was still living her old life, just as it had been in the time before the turmoil. There was, however, one single difference — though she continued to attend her old school located at Ninth street, 6, on Vasilievsky Island, she now commuted by streetcar.

Sania and Valentina attended Dowager Empress Maria Fyodrovna Girls' School, a prestigious public institution. It had been the fervent wish of Maria that her children go to ordinary schools, as she herself had, and not to seminaries or the schools attached to churches as was customary for the children of priests. But as her children matured, the wild streak that each possessed surfaced, and they became increasingly uncontrollable. Even the serene Father Valerian, though he initially agreed with his wife on her choice of schools, eventually agonized over the ineffectiveness of such educational policies.

One day, when they had a moment alone, he brought up the subject. "I don't mean to scold you for sending the children to ordinary schools instead of church schools," he said. "After all, I went along with the plan. I also know it's impossible to force our ideas on our children. Nevertheless, if we were to send our children to schools attached to churches, Christian traditions would prevail. Regardless of any changes in the world outside, our children would still have an education based on Christian values. But in ordinary schools—to an extent we can hardly imagine—children are left to drift on the tossing seas of life. I thought we made the right choice for them, but it seems we didn't. All a person can do now is pray that the children stay on the path of righteousness."

Matushka Maria, who had been listening in silence, uttered the last words, "It's too late for that now."

It was the custom at Valentina's school to begin each day with a prayer. Each morning at assembly, before the start of classes, an upper-class girl would read a prayer, after which the students, in groups of six, would approach the principal and bow deeply toward her.

The homeroom teacher responsible for each class was called *klassnaya dama* or "class lady." She taught no courses, and her sole duties were to keep an eye on her students and to perform certain administrative tasks. The most important of the *dama*'s duties was to give a report each week to the parents or guardians on the study progress and deportment of each student in her charge. Course teachers changed every year, but the student's *dama* stayed with her students, each year moving up to the next grade with her charges. Valentina's *dama*, who bore the hyphenated name Tolstaya-Miroslavskaya, was the daughter of aristocrats and had newly graduated from a normal school for women. Although she was not a great beauty, Valentina's *dama* was tall and carried herself gracefully. She was also accommodating of the rascally young

Valentina. Whenever Valentina played the imp or teased one of her course instructors, her *dama* would look the other way instead of scolding her.

Russia was at war with Germany, but German language classes were still being taught at the school. As one might expect, enrollment in the German class was low, and a great deal of teasing was directed at the instructors. The favored object of Valentina's teasing was a certain male teacher of German in his late thirties. A native German, he struggled to master the Russian language and occasionally committed hilariously funny grammatical errors. Valentina did imitations of his German-inflected Russian in mock serious tones that sent the other students into gales of laughter.

Although French and German were compulsory courses at the girls' school, English was not offered. Maria, who spared no expense for her children's education, paid an English tutor to teach Valentina, who, like her mother, had a gift for languages. Valentina never imagined that the English she was studying would one day stand her in good stead in Canada and the United States and all the stations on her voyage. Although Valentina loved foreign languages, Russian literature was her favorite. Even before encountering Dostoevsky in her class-reading assignments, Valentina had already read most of his chief works, though admittedly she had failed to fully grasp the ideas on which they were founded. For some reason, she felt a community of feeling with the central characters of Dostoevsky's works, and she was able to sympathize with their sad desperation. It excited her to learn that Dostoevsky had written *Crime and Punishment* in lodgings near where she now lived in Sennaya Square.

Sania's reaction, on the other hand, was one of scorn. "Oh, he's a little too gloomy. And besides, one gets bored reading him. The characters are sick in the head, and a lot of them are out-and-out weirdoes. I couldn't stand it if I thought that Russians were all like that. You know... like those silly fools in Gogol." At the time, Valentina didn't realize that this was the response of most Russians. Her opinion of Dostoevsky was so completely different from her sister's that she had difficulty reconciling them. If Sania's view is right, then why are the works of Dostoevsky and Gogol considered modern classics on a par with Tolstoy's *War and Peace* or *Anna Karenina*? No matter what Sania might say, once Valentina began a novel by Dostoevsky, she was carried along willy-nilly by its driving force and couldn't stop reading until she'd reached the end.

After the war started, public dancing, except for lessons at school, was prohibited. Almost all forms of entertainment were either forbidden or targeted for self-restraint. It was the opinion of the state that entertainment was not acceptable when soldiers were fighting on the front lines.

The Borotinski home likewise adopted a wartime footing. A big map had been put up on the wall of the new kitchen with pins, with little Russian flags attached to them, showing where the Russian Army's front lines were. This was before the era of the radio, so Nicholas and Valentina would peruse newspaper reports and then adjust the flag positions accordingly.

In the beginning, the little flags advanced on Austria, but soon enough, they bogged down in the vicinity of Poland. For a while, Valentina's flags moved back and forth over the surface of the map for no particular reason that she could conceive and then suddenly retreated as the German Army attacked in force. Rumors spread that the Russian General Samsonov had attempted suicide. The day was November 24, 1914.

Thereafter, the flag pins virtually stopped moving. The newspaper slogan, "Victory will be ours," rang hollow in the face of General Samsonov's miserable rout. Valentina read that the war on the Eastern Front had cost Russia 100,000 war dead and 100,000 prisoners of war. The criticism was aimed, however, not at General Samsonov but at the Russian Army's lack of equipment with which to combat Germany's well-trained and modern army.

At the same time, on the Western Front, Russia's ally France desperately needed reinforcements in order to maintain its position. Prince Mikhail, commander-in-chief of the Russian Army, deployed two brigades to the Prussian Eastern Front with the intention of dividing the German Army into two. Russia drew attention away from the Western Front and saved Paris at the cost of these two brigades.

It was becoming clear to Valentina that it would be a war of long duration and steady attrition and that Russia's prospects for victory were not bright. Although populated by a Slavic people, Bulgaria decided that its interests would best be served by allying itself with Turkey. The other smaller nations followed suit, siding with one camp or another.

In the late nineteenth and early twentieth centuries, middle-class youths in Russia were turning to France for aesthetic knowledge and to Germany for technological knowledge. While some people held that the dependence on German-imported goods was too extensive, the fact was that the quality of German products was way above its competitors. No one imagined that Russians were capable of manufacturing comparable items.

As for the French influence, imported social and aesthetic theory made the ability to read and write French indispensable. Not only was the French language taught in schools, but also most middle-class parents saw that their children received tuition in French at home.

It was common for wealthy people to send their children to Western Europe for study, and when they returned to Russia, these children sought to enlighten their fellow Russians with the knowledge they had cultivated in the West. In the eyes of these young people, Russia was a hopelessly backward country, crippled by entrenched superstition and prejudice.

The children had absorbed the philosophy and moral values of the countries they visited along with the language.

In early twentieth-century imperial Russia, intellectuals who adopted Western liberalist ideas and awakened to their personal, social, and political responsibilities were called *intelligentsia*. On one hand, the Russian intelligentsia recognized theoretically the equality of all men, but they did not transfer this knowledge onto the role that their ancestors had played or the roles that they themselves were still playing. Rather, they continued the traditional relationship between landowner and peasant long after the liberal Tsar Alexander II had emancipated the serfs in 1861. Valentina had heard these historical events from her parents. At first, Alexander earned much good will among the people, but after 1866, his rule became increasingly autocratic. This stimulated considerable revolutionary and terrorist activity that eventually culminated in the tsar's assassination.

History does not record anyone, not even the radical ideologues and novelists, who refused the money thus created by peasant labor. No less a figure than the humanist Alexander Herzen himself is said to have raised capital to go abroad by selling off a considerable portion of his lands and serfs. After leaving his homeland, Herzen published numerous revolutionary tracts, such as *Russian Socialism,* which were smuggled into Russia.

In 1906, Tsar Nicholas II appointed Pyotr Stolypin as prime minister. Stolypin instituted liberal reforms for agricultural land use whereby farmers could privatize property formerly held by the village commune. By this means, he hoped to win the support of the rural population and stabilize it politically. Although grain production rose dramatically and a nascent class of well-to-do farmers emerged, Stolypin's methodology was, in fact, not altogether benign. He undercut the goodwill he won on the agricultural front by establishing military tribunals, which had the power to summarily sentence a suspected terrorist to death by hanging. Many activists met this fate. It was no surprise for Valentina's family when in 1911 Stolypin was assassinated.

Hoping to share in the exercise of power in the new age that was about to dawn, liberal and radical ideologues returned home in ever greater numbers to their Mother Russia.

CHAPTER II

Cousins

War brought drastic changes to the city of Petrograd. Many stores and businesses operated by foreign nationals were shuttered, as their owners fled hastily back to their native Germany or Austria. Throughout the city, walls got plastered with jingoist posters and patriotic exhortations. Long lists of the names of the dead and wounded were also posted. Somber memorial services soon replaced the gaiety of dance halls and theaters. Every Russian, young or old, radical or conservative, was, for the moment, caught up in a mood of patriotism and would, in the event an enemy invaded Russia, gladly lay down his life for his mother country.

In the Borotinski household, Russia's climate of social turmoil had also made its impression upon the family. Then came more news in a letter from Modest. He informed the family that he planned to marry a cousin with whom he had fallen in love when she had been living under his parents' roof.

Father Valerian had four brothers and one sister. Valentina had four paternal uncles, one aunt, and many cousins. The eldest of Valentina's uncles was Uncle Nicholas who, in his prime, served as a deacon at the church attached to the Marble Palace in Petrograd. Uncle Nicholas was blessed with a loving wife, who had died an untimely death. Before she died, however, she bore him four daughters and a son. Uncle Nicholas's wife's unmarried younger sister, who had been living with the family, remained to care for the children.

This living arrangement, however, had a ruinous effect on Uncle Nicholas's reputation. As a widowed deacon of the Orthodox faith, he was forbidden to live in the same house with an unmarried woman. He was also forbidden to marry her. On various occasions, his brothers urged him to part with his wife's sister, but he could not bear to do it. At length, in order to preserve the dignity of the Marble Palace, the church banished Nicholas to a church in the village called Valgovitsi. His sister-in-law went with him.

Valentina had visited Uncle Nicholas's house in the village and had a wonderful time with her cousins. In the countryside, education lasted only through the elementary school years. The eldest of the four cousins, Svetlana, however, wanted to continue to learn. When she entered her teens, she told her father that she wanted to study in the capital. Nicholas then made arrangements with Matushka Maria to take Svetlana into her house and teach her skills that would qualify the young girl for a good job. The girls would each, in turn, be cared for similarly. Valentina's family had moved to a larger house in the heart of the capital, and they were now financially comfortable, making such generosity possible.

In the case of Svetlana, all went tremendously well. Quiet, obedient, and possessed of an unassuming nature, Svetlana soon found herself a teaching job at an orphanage. Even after moving into an apartment of her own, she would often return to spend holidays with Matushka Maria and Father Valerian, for whom she had gained an abiding affection.

The second daughter, Nina, was the exact opposite of Svetlana. She liked excitement, and for this reason, Valentina and the other children were drawn to her. Matushka Maria had considered Nina a respectable girl just like her elder sister until she received a letter from her son Modest informing her that he and Nina were deeply in love and planned to get married.

This scandalous piece of news raised a storm of controversy in the Borotinski household. To begin with, marriage between first cousins was prohibited by the church, but what had upset Maria most was that they had been carrying on right under her nose! Father Valerian was obliged to report the matter to Modest's godfather, the archbishop of St. Isaac's Cathedral, who was charged with administration of the Archdiocese of Petrograd. A directive immediately went out to all the churches in the archdiocese, forbidding anyone to marry the two. Nina was brusquely sent back to her father in the country.

Uncle Nicholas never again showed his face at the Borotinski's household, and all contact between the cousins came to a halt. Valentina learned every detail of the affair from their gossipy Polish housekeeper, and she sympathized with Nina and her uncle's family. Modest deeply resented the treatment she had received at the hands of his parents and, as a gesture of defiance, stopped writing home.

Amidst all the drama in the Borotinski's household, the war continued on inexorably. Tens of thousands of lives were sacrificed, and a pall of despair settled over Russia. Apparently, only Tsarina Alexandra believed the tsar's conviction that if he led Russia into battle, he could change the course of the war.

On August 24, 1915, Tsar Nicholas assumed personal command of all of Russia's military forces from Grand Duke

Mikhail, who took responsibility for failure to turn the tide of war. The tsar came to the decision, without consulting his cabinet, that he should leave for the front immediately, accompanied by Crown Prince Alexis who, he thought, as future emperor, should see a battlefield as part of his education. Tsar Nicholas was confident that it would raise troop morale and have a favorable effect on the outcome of the war when the crown prince appeared before them astride his white warhorse. And it did, for a short time, but in the end, leaving the capital was the biggest mistake that the tsar could have made. The empress, acting as the emperor's proxy in his absence, administered government in Petrograd with the assistance of his ministers. Adventurers arrived one after the other to curry favor with Rasputin, who enjoyed the complete confidence of the empress, who accepted and dismissed palace personnel at Rasputin's whim.

During the war years, Valentina's one comfort was that her parents permitted her to have friends over to the house in the evening to enjoy music, dancing, and sharing their thoughts. Amidst so much dark news, these happy evenings were a great comfort to her.

One day, Valentina was riding through Nevsky Prospect on the streetcar, and she saw, in a quarter lined with liquor shops and bars, her cousin Nina. She stood among a group of well-turned-out girls, and though not behaving at all rudely, the girls appeared to be calling out to male office workers, army officers, university students, and even older men who had gathered there. And among them Nina, her favorite cousin, was smoking a cigarette. The realization that Nina, with whom until just recently she had lived in the same house, was now selling her body horrified Valentina.

Modest and Nina's love affair fell in the realm of taboo, and so for this reason, it was hushed up in front of the other children. As a consequence, there was no one in the family to whom Valentina could speak regarding what had happened. Each time she recalled seeing Nina standing there with the other girls, Valentina's conscience bothered her, for she felt that in her silence, she had acquiesced in Maria's banishment of Nina.

From the day Maria had forever shut poor Nina out of her heart, Valentina scrutinized her mother closely. For the duration of her life, Valentina could only hope that Nina would find the warmth of affection that Maria had so cruelly denied her and that Valentina had been too priggish to offer. After all, she could have jumped off the streetcar and run to her cousin . . . but she did not. Valentina never saw Nina again.

The Borotinski children came to know one more family of cousins, the children of Father Valerian's younger sister, Ekaterina. Valerian's mother had raised six children, five boys and one girl. Because his sweet-natured father, Fedot, chose not to scold them, Valerian's mother assumed the role of family disciplinarian; however, she doted on her only daughter, and Ekaterina grew up self-willed and proud.

Ekaterina eventually married a virtuous priest from a nearby town with whom she bore two boys and two girls. But her husband died young of tuberculosis, leaving their four children in her care.

The widowed Ekaterina now came, squeezing her four children somehow into her mother's cramped quarters. Misfortune had a negative effect on Ekaterina in that it made her even more arrogant. She became known within their circle of relatives as "the one best avoided."

Maria had not yet met her sister-in-law, but she pondered the rumors. *There cannot be anyone in the world as unpleasant as that*, she thought as she awaited the opportunity to finally visit Ekaterina. The day at last came when Maria arrived with her daughters to visit Ekaterina at her mother-in-law's apartment. Valentina was immensely pleased to finally meet her cousins. They welcomed her with open arms, and they soon became absorbed in play. However, Maria's visit was not so joyful. While Valentina's grandmother was in the kitchen making sandwiches and lemonade, Ekaterina spoke words that cut Maria to the quick, the content of which could neither be repeated nor redressed.

Maria was still boiling with rage when they arrived home, but Valerian, when he heard the terrible things said by Ekaterina, only replied, "Go easy with her. Poor thing. She's so unhappy."

Never again did the formidable Maria visit her sister-in-law Ekaterina. The link with Ekaterina's family was henceforth maintained only through Valerian and his mother. Except for the times when they visited their grandmother, Valentina could speak to her cousins only in the street. The ill will that festered between her mother and her aunt saddened Valentina because she liked her cousins very much. She was especially disappointed at not being able to talk with her cousin Andrei, who was just her age.

She bumped into him once on Nevsky Prospect and found herself saying, "Oh, it's you! How have you been?"

"OK," Andrei replied and averted his eyes. It seemed as if they both felt they were somehow betraying their mothers.

CHAPTER 12

Brother's Wife

New Year's Day, 1916, dawned on yet another day of war. Russia was still engaged on the Eastern Front with German troops, who were looking over their shoulders toward their comrades on the Western Front who were caught up in a prolonged and gruesome battle with France at Verdun. This cataclysmic yet geographically confined exercise in horror earned Verdun the epithet, "Blood pump of the world." However, amidst this relentless stream of gory battlefield reports, an announcement came by mail to the Borotinski household of a circumstance promising private joy.

Modest, who had not been in contact with his family since Maria had quashed his efforts to marry his cousin Nina, had written to tell them that he had met and fallen in love with a girl at an army hospital who was as pretty and as sweet as an angel.

Modest sent a second letter reporting that he had arranged for leave and would arrive home soon to marry his fiancée. Because the war made it difficult to assemble a proper wedding feast in Petrograd, Matushka Maria decided to limit the wedding guest list to the immediate family only. Maria pulled out all the stops in orchestrating a warm welcome for her eldest son's fiancée. She began by delivering a lengthy sermon to Valentina and her sister, in which she warned them of the dire consequences that would ensue from any mention of a certain previous love affair. Furthermore, even if they didn't like Modest's fiancée, they still must mind their manners and be attentive to her needs.

The day of Modest's return came at last. Exhausted from their long journey, he and his fiancée, Olga, hired a carriage to take them from the train station to Father Valerian's rectory.

Maria regretted the heartbreak she had caused her son over his previous romantic relationship and was thrilled that he had come back. This time, she intended to go about cautiously, giving her blessings to her son and his fiancée. For his part, though Father Valerian never stopped smiling, he kept a vigilant eye trained on Olga. Indeed, she was a creature of angelic beauty, but eventually, the family learned that Olga had a wild streak in her.

Initially, Olga had been reticent to speak, but as the days passed and she gradually began to open up to Modest's family, they discovered that she smoked cigarettes, played the guitar, and had an alluring singing voice. As Modest's leave was short, Father Valerian married the couple in a small ceremony, after which they shared a light repast before going to seek the blessings of the bride's parents, who lived in an outlying town. Modest's leave was soon over, so he entrusted his bride to his parents' care and returned to his regiment.

Modest had said that Olga came from a poor family, yet she would weave elaborate fictions about her youth that could hardly have happened to anyone growing up in poverty. Valentina and Sania were initially curious to hear the story of her life, but when they realized that it was largely make-believe, they did their best to avoid being roped into playing the role of the credulous audience.

And it wasn't just the wild stories. Olga's whole outlook on life appeared out of tune with the Borotinski's domestic atmosphere of stiff and reticent austerity. In her new life, Olga discovered a measure of freedom that she exercised by getting up late and spending hours on her makeup. In the afternoon, she played her guitar and sang or, if she had an audience, told outlandish stories that she attributed to her personal history.

When Olga sang, however, even Maria, albeit with her ingrained distaste for pleasure, would stop work to enjoy Olga's singing. Everyone agreed that Olga had a very fine voice and that her phrasing was masterful. When she sang a folk song or a romantic ballad, everyone, even within hearing distance, was held spellbound.

One of Father Valerian's parishioners, the elderly Marchioness Ukhtomskaya, a pious Christian, would suddenly appear at Maria's door, extravagantly dressed, her withered face encrusted with powder, and stay for hours chattering away in her high-pitched voice. One day, she appeared and pestered Maria to let her see for herself this new wife of Modest. The marchioness told Maria that Olga was a great beauty who could sing so sweetly that even the birds stopped to listen. Resigning herself to the inevitable gossip to which Olga would now be subjected, Maria grudgingly granted her wish.

Olga entered the room, and Maria introduced them. Then, in her screeching voice, the marchioness offered formal congratulations for Olga's marriage. She then asked Olga to sing one of her songs for her. After looking to Maria for a nod, Olga brought out her guitar and began to sing. The song she sang was a *chansonette*, a type of French love song—one that neither the marchioness nor Maria had ever heard—that was popular at the time in nightclubs in the capital. Olga sang her song with a passion and intimacy that one would not expect to hear in a parish priest's rectory. Maria was speechless. The marchioness, who had listened politely down to the very last measure, a stricken smile on her face, praised Olga's beautiful voice, then hurriedly made her apologies and left.

Had Maria's daughter-in-law deliberately chosen this song out of a mischievous curiosity to see just how disturbed the passionate lyrics might make the old woman feel? Maria, who was innocent in the ways of the world, could not imagine why Olga would sing such an inappropriate song. Maria began to worry about Olga's wild side.

Nicholas's visit had occurred on a weekend, and he spent much of every weekend in conversation with Olga. Maria worried about the developing friendship between Nicholas and Olga. He would soon be coming home from officers' training school. Surely, he wouldn't make overtures to his own brother's wife, would he? Maria didn't know. Perhaps it hadn't been such a good idea to keep Olga with them, after all. Maria had learned from Modest's affair with his cousin Nina that it was best not to give young people an opportunity to find trouble.

This was not the only trouble that caused Maria to worry. The war was not going well. By the autumn of 1916, the number of Russian casualties and prisoners of war had risen to five million. The language of revolutionaries was now shouting for the overthrow of church and state, and their voices had become more strident and incendiary. The times were perilous, and Maria hesitated to mention to Father

Valerian yet another matter, for it would only increase her husband's worries. As it turned out, there was no need for Maria to bring up the subject. Valerian himself made the announcement to the family that Nicholas's cadet school had abruptly scheduled his graduation ahead of time. Nicholas would soon be drafted and sent to the front as a member of a brigade of reinforcements.

Valerian tried to comfort the family. "*Matushka*, it is not we alone who are sad. There are many mothers and fathers, wives and children who are just as sad as we are."

Maria made no overt response. Then, unable to bear her sorrow any longer, she rose and left the room, followed by Sania and Valentina who went to their rooms and cried. Father Valerian remained alone with his thoughts. In Modest's room, Olga was singing a song to the accompaniment of her guitar. She did not yet know that Nicholas's draft notice had arrived.

Toward the close of the year, on December 17, 1916, Valentina's family heard the news that Rasputin had been assassinated. Through his uncanny ability to stop the bleeding of the hemophiliac Crown Prince Alexis, Rasputin had acquired unprecedented entry into the imperial court, gaining great favor with the empress. Besides misusing the favors that the imperial court bestowed on him, Rasputin was also rumored to have staged sex orgies at his home. Because of this, Prince Felix Yusupov and two of his confederates assassinated him in order to protect the reputation of the royal family.

On the designated day Prince Felix Yusupov invited Rasputin to his opulent mansion in Petrograd alongside the Moika Canal. Rasputin was given wine laced with potassium cyanide and cakes, but it had no apparent effect on him. Rasputin was then shot twice, once by Yusupov himself. Badly wounded, he was bound with rope and pushed into a dark crevice in the iced-over Neva River.

There was joy in the streets of the capital at the news of the death of the demonic character, and the assassins were acclaimed national heroes. The empress, however, demanded the culprits' heads, but after a list of Rasputin's crimes was read at a meeting of the imperial family members, the option of capital punishment was rejected.

In the end, Felix, scion of the wealthy Yusupov family, wealthier even than the world's wealthiest monarch, Nicholas II, was banished from Petrograd with accomplice Prince Dmitry and exiled to Persia.

CHAPTER 13

February Revolution

One morning, in February 1917, a few months after the news that Rasputin had been assassinated, Sania and Valentina were getting ready to go to school when Father Valerian, returning from Matins, suddenly stopped them. "We'd better not send the girls to school today," he said. "They say something's going on in the streets. Crowds are gathering, and the trolleys aren't running."

Valentina, who now did not have to go to school, went into the church garden, where she found other children who had likewise stayed home for the same reason. They were all intensely curious to know what was happening and considered going out into Nevsky Prospect to mingle with the people. One of the boys suggested they climb the church's highest bell tower to see what they could see. Valentina followed them up into the bell tower. At Pascha, the boys were permitted to climb the towers to ring the bells, so most of the children knew the way up.

Looking down over Nevsky Prospect, they could see that a corridor was open in the middle of the avenue so that trucks carrying soldiers and sailors could get by, but both sides were packed with marching demonstrators. One student climbed up a telephone pole and began shouting something, but no one was listening. The crowds continued to swell as the people advanced in eerie silence toward the Winter Palace.

At this point, Valentina had not yet realized that what she was witnessing was a revolution. She had presumed that people in the midst of a revolution would be running around and shooting each other. She did not recognize the swell of people and their silent advance on the Winter Palace as revolutionary. But what she had seen was, in fact, the February Revolution. After having watched the demonstrators from the bell tower, she heard from others that there had been rioting on Nevsky Prospect and on Vasilievsky Island. Looters had thrown stones, shattering the windows of bakeries throughout the city, beginning with Filipov's, whose delicious piroshki Valentina and her family loved. She later learned from her parents that the Cossack Horse Guard had been called out.

These events occurred on February 23, 1917, of the Julian calendar. Trusting that order would be restored to the capital, Tsar Nicholas II had set out for Tsarskoye Selo, his estate outside the city, but since trains could not travel in that direction, he was forced to return to Pskov.

On March 15, 1917, the State Assembly, or Duma, accepted the abdication of the tsar who ceded the throne to his younger brother, Grand Duke Mikhail. The grand duke refused it. Thus, the 304-year rule of the Romanov Dynasty over the Russian Empire ended.

Anarchy reigned in the capital. Transportation was paralyzed. The supply of food and fuel ground to a halt. An interim government under Prince Lvov was established, but the situation remained out of control. In July, leadership of the provisional government passed to Alexander Kerensky, the minister of justice. Kerensky was a thoroughgoing liberal and an eloquent speaker, but he was unwilling to renounce the war, and this eventually led to his downfall.

Describing it as a measure to assure the personal safety of Nicholas and his family, the provisional government had the royal family confined at Tsarskoye Selo.

Thus, the curtain fell on act one of the Russian Revolution. Casualties were surprisingly few — with 1,443 civilians dead, 60 army officers wounded, and 869 soldiers dead or wounded. For this reason, the February Revolution was sometimes called the Bloodless Revolution.

Kerensky promised Russia's allies that Russian troops would remain in the field until the day Russians won over the Germans. German leaders, however, aware of the changing situation in Russia and with the aim of exacerbating the internal dissension, arranged for a "sealed train" to carry Lenin and other revolutionaries from neutral Switzerland through Germany to Russia.

Lenin, who had received reports of the February Revolution, arrived at the Finland Station in Petrograd on April 16, 1917. Wearing a cloth hat and carrying an elegant bouquet of flowers in his arms, Lenin gave a speech to the detail of sailors who had come to welcome him.

"Sailors, comrades, the people need peace. The people need bread. The people need land. But the government gives you war. It gives you starvation, and it gives you no food. The land remains in the hands of the landholders. Sailors, comrades, we must fight for the revolution, for the final objective, for total victory of the proletariat. Long live the world socialist revolution!"

Lenin, leader of the radical Communist faction known as the Bolsheviks, condemned the war against Germany and began to propagandize for Communism among the troops and peasants. On the battlefield, war-weariness was spreading little by little as the front line fell back, while at home, peasants and workers had begun to loot factories and banks, and turmoil was gradually deepening.

In the wake of the February Revolution, the transport system had broken down. Day by day, food became more difficult to obtain. Valentina's family stood in lines formed to buy a loaf of bread. To secure rations, one sometimes had to wait in line from early morning until noon. What was even more serious than the scarcity of food, however, was the breakdown of public morale. Social order and personal dignity, which had been observed in peacetime, were now lost. Looting shops or the homes of the wealthy now became a common occurrence.

Even the churches were not exempted from the looting. A band of soldiers suddenly barged into the Uspensky precincts without a search warrant and demanded that Father Valerian open the doors of the church. Rumors had been spread that priests were using churches to conceal food supplies they had swindled from the people. The soldiers did not find the foodstuffs they were looking for, and so they turned next to the homes of the clergy to continue their search. There was nothing for the soldiers to find, but time and again, bands of testy soldiers appeared at Father Valerian's door and stomped through the house in their dirty boots, searching. Then one day, a soldier came and asked to be put up for the night. It was a time of fear and confusion, and Valerian simply could not turn him away. All the rooms in the Borotinski home were occupied, however, and there was none for the soldier who would have to make do with the bathtub.

Olga, who had been staying in Modest's room since his return to the front, woke up hearing noises in the night. It sounded as if someone was walking around very slowly. She arose, turned on the light, and crept stealthily in the direction of the bathroom where the noises seemed to originate. There she saw the soldier, fully dressed, lumbering heavily about, holding a rifle in his hands. Olga hurried back to wake the family, and they all gathered around the samovar on the dinner table. Realizing he had been found out, the soldier responded with the nonsensical explanation that he had been looking for the bathroom. They insisted he leave immediately. Who knows what horrible thing might have happened if Olga hadn't awakened! Everyone, not least of all Father Valerian, felt shivers run down their spines at the thought of it.

It was summertime, and had there not been a revolution with its attendant confusion, it was the time of year when they would have gone on their yearly summer vacation. For Valentina, summer was the season of fond memories of travel to Finland, which Valentina had visited so many times; Kiev, the capital of Ukraine, where she had gone the summer she turned ten; and Crimea, where she had been when the war broke out. But Russia was no longer a place for vacations. Even in neighboring Finland, the effects of the revolution were being felt, so they were told.

Valentina read the newspaper report on August 6 that Nicholas II and his family were sent from Tsarskoye Selo to Tobolsk in Siberia. This reflected Kerensky's concern that Tsarskoye Selo was now too dangerous for them to stay. In the capital, the Bolsheviks were calling for the execution of the Romanovs. Valentina was horrified.

A young factory worker who sometimes came to attend services brought Father Valerian a handbill that was printed over with communist propaganda. The propaganda read as follows:

"The workers of the world are now united. The aristocrats, the bourgeoisie, the clerics, they who over the centuries have deceived the people are the people's enemies. The clerics have oppressed the poor and the masses with their talk of a god that doesn't exist. They say you can go to a heaven that doesn't exist. Die, you parasites! Die, you liars feeding on the blood of the people!"

For Father Valerian and his family, the tensions of life in the city were becoming more painful to bear. It was as if a river had risen to the danger level and might at any moment overflow its banks, or so it seemed to Father Valerian. He now wondered if it would be best to send Matushka Maria and his daughters to safety in the south of Russia. A great number of people had already gone to the south. He had been told that food was still abundant there, and life was still peaceful. Furthermore, he had heard that the Cossacks, whose homeland it was, were thought to be opposed to the revolution.

The handbill with the propaganda settled the matter; he would send his wife and daughters south as soon as possible. Matushka Maria did not oppose the plan. They assumed that leaving Petrograd was a temporary measure, but just in case, they packed their most important documents and enough clothes to last for the time being. Then they dug a hole beneath a tree in the garden and buried their silverware and porcelain to keep until they returned.

Because it was too heavy, they decided to leave the family album behind also. Valentina would later regret that they had not at least ripped out the photos that were most important to them.

The Borotinski relatives were astounded with disbelief when they learned of the plan to seek safety in the south. Everyone thought that the current period of confusion would soon resolve itself. It was ridiculous to leave the capital where they had lived so long and enjoyed such happiness. But Valerian and Maria's determination was unshakable.

Instead of going with the family on their journey to the south, Olga left Maria and the others and made her way instead to the town where Modest's detachment was stationed. Nicholas joined a heavy artillery unit at the front. Father Valerian's position obliged him to stay with his congregation, so he remained in the capital. Maria decided on Ekaterinodar as their place of refuge and readied the family for the trip there. She had chosen her Ekaterinodar because her daughters' French teacher, Madame Simon, wished to accompany them with her son Alfred. Madame Simon's brother-in-law lived in Ekaterinodar and had promised to secure a house for them.

They began their journey in September 1917. With heavy, low-hanging clouds hiding the sky and an occasional raindrop spattering on the foot-worn paving stones, a horse and carriage carrying Matushka Maria and her party headed for Moscow Station, where a train had began building steam to carry them south.

CHAPTER 14

Ekaterinodar

Ekaterinodar (now Krasnodar) sat on the banks of the Kuban River near the Sea of Azov and reigned as the capital of Kuban Region. Valentina was amazed to discover that she could buy whatever foods she wanted in Ekaterinodar—even white bread, which she hadn't eaten since the outbreak of the revolution!

What a difference! When they boarded the train, the sky over Petrograd was overcast, the air was unseasonably chilly, and a cold rain was beginning to fall; after the chill of Petrograd, here in the South, dazzling sunshine warmed their bodies and souls. Food was abundant. People greeted them amiably. The Cossack soldiery was friendly. Civil order still prevailed, and it was apparent that the government maintained the respect of the citizens. They did not make arbitrary searches, nor did the citizens loot the shops as there had been in Petrograd. People could go to sleep at night assured of their safety.

Together with Madame Simon and her son Alfred, Matushka Maria and her two daughters settled in a rented house in the middle of town arranged for them by Madame Simon's brother-in-law.

About half of the people in the Kuban Region were of Cossack origin. The rest were *inogorodnye* "resident outsiders," whose ranks the Borotinskis and Madame Simon and her son had now joined.

Valentina entered Ekaterinodar Second Girls' School for her final year of high school. The school possessed a distinctly populist and liberal ambience which appealed to Valentina. Besides the indigenous Cossacks and the Russian girls who, like Valentina, had fled the turmoil of the North, there were also Armenians, Jews, and Georgians in her class. Sania had finished high school and was now studying at a nursing school, hoping to work eventually at an army hospital.

While Matushka Maria was settling her daughters into this temporary haven in the South, Lenin had began to engineer his Russian Revolution in earnest on October 25, old style; hence, "the October Revolution."

Lenin had been biding his time since an abortive *putsch* against the provisional government in the summer of 1917. Then he learned that A. F. Kerensky, premier of the provisional government, had decided to launch a preemptive strike against the Bolsheviks by arresting some of their leaders. Lenin immediately ordered the Red Guard to march to the Winter Palace. Bolshevik sympathizers aboard the cruiser *Aurora* fired a signal round, and the attack commenced. The Bolsheviks swiftly occupied the Winter Palace, and led by Lenin, the Military Revolutionary Committee grasped political power. Kerensky fled Petrograd. The first socialist government thus came into existence.

To her horror, Maria learned that Lenin and Leon Trotsky now had the power of life and death over those who had previously occupied positions of authority, responsibility, and influence. Lenin and his associates had began to go after aristocrats, the military, the police, and clergy, such as Valentina's father, and now treated them as criminals.

Numerous members of the aristocracy, former government officials, and clergy were summarily shot or placed in confinement. The purge extended even to the intelligentsia, who, despite having propagandized for the revolution, were suspected of being turncoats and forced to flee or be sent to detention centers in the north or in Siberia.

The new officials of the revolutionary government were either incompetent or unfair. Some, in fact, were dishonest and irresponsible. Many citizens scorned the Bolsheviks, but their contempt was outweighed by their fear of them. They allowed themselves to be carried along on the tide of events, hoping against hope that things would somehow get sorted out and the old ways would magically be restored.

Whenever news concerning the October Revolution reached their ears, Maria and her daughters were desperate to find out what might have befallen Father Valerian. Then one day, there came a knock at the door, and they opened it to discover Nicholas and Valerian, who had come with just the clothes on their backs. Things had gotten worse in the capital. Valerian had been on the point of running for his life into the countryside when Nicholas showed up, having given up on the army, which had been paralyzed by the Bolshevik Revolution; together they started out for Ekaterinodar. They rejoiced the safe family reunion for a while.

Nicholas decided to join a White-Russian volunteer army organized by the Kuban Cossacks. The Cossacks were against the Bolsheviks.

Father Valerian spent a few days with his family and then went to see the bishop in charge of the Kuban Region, who sent him to help an ailing priest in a distant village. Valerian had brought news that Madame Simon's husband would soon be arriving from Petrograd, so Maria prepared to move out.

Valentina realized from her father's descriptions of the situation in the capital that civil war was inevitable. He said that it was highly unlikely that they would return to Petrograd. With a rush of nostalgia for her old school and classmates, Valentina wondered what everyone was doing now. Why had the world come crashing down around them? Would life ever be normal again?

The Bolshevik Revolution turned into a violent upheaval and shed the blood of millions. The Bolshevik-led Red Army pitted against various anti-Bolshevik White Armies in a massive civil war that fought on the perimeter of the far-flung lands of Russia. General L. G. Kornilov, leader of the antirevolutionary White Army in European Russia, the core of which made up of southern Russian Cossacks, launched a campaign against the Bolshevik Reds.

Many concluded that things would only grow worse and now made arrangements to leave the country. The Borotinskis, however, whose three men necessarily had to stay behind, decided to remain in Russia a little longer in the hopes of a White victory on the battlefield.

When the Bolsheviks, led by Lenin, seized political power, the imperialist-geopolitical underpinning of Russia's participation in a war against foreign powers became meaningless. The enemies of the Bolsheviks were not nation states but the social classes that preyed on the proletariat: the aristocrats, the bourgeoisie, and the intelligentsia. Lenin directed Trotsky to enter into peace negotiations with

Russia's adversaries, and on December 3, 1917, a conference was convened at Brest-Litovsk.

At the height of the Bolshevik Revolution, Valentina's eldest brother Modest, who was serving on the front line in the Crimea, was arrested by the Bolsheviks for fighting in the White army and imprisoned along with other officers of the former Imperial Army.

Modest's wife Olga, who had followed him to the front as an army nurse, was able to visit him often in prison. She learned from Modest that the "People's Court" before which he and the other officers were being tried was a mere charade performed to articulate the politically expedient notion that criminals, traitors, and the bourgeoisie had infiltrated the military. Those found guilty were sentenced to detainment in a labor camp and confiscation of all their property. In fact, large numbers of them were disposed of in other ways, to one of which Olga bore witness.

While Modest was imprisoned, awaiting for the show trial, Olga would occasionally go to a Black Sea beach to swim. One day, when she had swum out farther than she normally did, she felt something brush her leg. She swam down to the seabed to see what had touched her. At first she didn't understand, but then she raced for shore, screaming as she went. Sprouting from the bottom of the sea were countless corpses. Their feet tied to large stones, they appeared to be standing in the water, their hands gently undulating with the to-and-fro lurch of the sea. For several days, Olga kept to her bed; thereafter, she never went swimming in the Black sea.

It was Modest's good fortune to have attended a technical college before the war, for the skills he acquired resulted in his being judged useful to the Russian people, and he was released. Accompanied by Olga, who was still traumatized by the horrific tableau she had witnessed at the bottom of the sea, he escaped from Crimea and set out for Ekaterinodar to join his family. Maria and the girls were happy to see Modest and Olga.

Though still a schoolgirl, Valentina volunteered her services after school at the White Army hospital. She helped prepare meals for the wounded or collected scraps of cloth for bandages. Help was needed everywhere.

At length, Madame Simon's husband arrived, and Maria and her daughters moved to new quarters in order to make room for him.

In February 1918, Lenin moved the capital from Petrograd to Moscow, and at the Party Congress that year, the Bolsheviks changed the party name from the Russian Social Democratic Labor Party to the Russian Communist Party.

The boom of artillery was now audible in Ekaterinodar during engagements between the Red Army, which had fought its way out of Crimea, and the White Volunteer Army of Kuban Cossacks, who were being driven north.

One day, as Valentina was at the station helping to distribute food to the soldiers, she suddenly noticed that the White Volunteer Army was being evacuated from the city. She wished it weren't so, but she could only conclude that the White Army forces in town were no longer strong enough to hold their own against the Reds and were leaving to join up with the main force under General Kornilov. With no troops to protect them, she wondered what would happen to the citizens of Ekaterinodar.

Not only was the White Volunteer Army fighting a desperate defensive war, but it also had not been issued winter clothing, and it was a particularly cold winter. Some of the volunteers marched off wrapped in rags, while others, slightly better off, had bundled themselves in blankets brought from home.

Among the partisans who fled from the Red Army were Valentina's brothers, Nicholas and Modest. During the Red Army's offensive and the White Army's retreat, Nicholas contracted pneumonia, and thanks to his loyal Cossack orderly who took care of him in his own home at great risk to himself and family, Nicholas managed to survive! He rejoined the White Army guerrillas after he recovered. For some months, this guerrilla army fought in snow and ice. Many suffered from hunger and fatigue. They lost hope and died one after another.

The severe fighting involved the retreating guerrillas, who fought against the Red Army. Their quest to join Kornilov was called The Ice Campaign. Only one thousand soldiers survived and succeeded in joining up with the main army of General Kornilov. Among them were Modest and Nicholas. Those who survived were later given a badge that depicted a sword embellished with a crown of thorns. That recalled the crown of thorns put on Jesus Christ when he was crucified. It also symbolized the suffering that these fighting men had to endure during this campaign against the atheist Bolsheviks.

In one of these battles, Nicholas displayed particular valor. On that day, he had overslept and awoke to find his White Army comrades being routed by a unit of Red Army cavalry. He dashed down in his underwear to where the artillery was parked and, rallying the men, fired round after round at the enemy cavalry, forcing them to retreat. Nicholas's superior officers put him up for a citation, but the act of heroism was judged to have been but one of many performed by the unit as a whole.

By April 1918, Valentina and her family could tell from the rumble of artillery and the crack of rifle fire that the battle to retake Ekaterinodar was now being fought at the very gates of the city. Everyone was certain that the White Army would carry the day, when rumor of a tragic happening quickly spread throughout the city. On April 13, General Kornilov was killed in an artillery barrage. The Red Army advanced on Ekaterinodar carrying the general's corpse. They had placed it on the bed of a truck, and they paraded it through the streets for all to see. Valentina did not go to see the corpse but cried bitterly when Maria told her that she had seen it personally.

Upon Kornilov's death, A. I. Denikin took command of the White Army and retreated with his troops into the Kuban Steppes to regroup. Thus, the war between the "Whites" and the "Reds" began in Southern Russia around the Don River. The war spread in Siberia as well.

Shortly before these events, Matushka Maria and her two daughters had changed their residence. They had moved not to cramped apartments but to an elegant mansion, the house of a wealthy merchant who was now residing outside Russia. The house had, in effect, been abandoned, but a friend of the merchant, certain that he could trust Maria, offered her the house to live in if she would care for it until the merchant returned.

Maria never asked the merchant's friend how the merchant had left Russia or where he had gone. But one thing was certain—he had left behind a treasure trove. Valentina knew she would never forget the many beautiful rooms in his grand mansion. No expense had been spared in the purchase of fine furniture, valuable paintings, closets full of the finest linen, imported tableware, crystal glassware, and porcelain vases, all of which were beheld by the Borotinskis with great amazement. But it was not a time for entertaining guests, and Maria never had the opportunity to use any of these borrowed treasures.

CHAPTER 15

The Red Army

Beginning in April 1918, Ekaterinodar was occupied by the Red Army for four months. The merchant's house in which the Borotinski women took up residence was both spacious and conspicuous; it immediately caught the eye of officials in the occupying Red Army. They commended the family to lodge a former factory worker who bore the title of People's Commissar. As a *matushka*, Maria had learned to deal skillfully with people of every social class when they came to see Father Valerian, and she was confident that she could reach an understanding with her lodger. She even believed that she and her daughters would remain safe, because they had a People's Commissar staying under their roof.

For the first few weeks of the occupation, the Red Army zealously swept the town for White Army sympathizers, who, for one reason or another, had remained behind. Some were wounded and could not keep up with their comrades, some were perhaps spies, and yet others had simply been left behind in the confusion of the White Army's withdrawal.

One of the latter was a Circassian named Sunbatt, with whom Sania had become infatuated. When Sania met him, he had managed to evade the Red Army's dragnet by hiding in somebody's house. Sania felt sorry for Sunbatt and wanted to do whatever she could to help him. After agonizing over what to do, Sania decided to go to the People's Commissar living in the Borotinski house and ask him to issue Sunbatt a fake Red Army ID card. The People's Commissar, who had told them stories about his past and was quite friendly with Maria and her daughters, agreed to do as Sania requested.

When Valentina learned from her sister what Sania had done, Valentina was astounded. "What are you doing? The commissar only agreed so he can capture Sunbatt."

"No, we're going to use a false name, not Sunbatt's real name, so it'll work out all right."

What an idiot! Valentina thought, doubting her own ears. "I can't believe any sister of mine could be so stupid." *How could anyone as intelligent as Sania not realize that the Red Army would surely investigate anyone asking for an ID card under a false name?* Besotted with love, Sania was apparently no longer in her right mind. Sania, as always, insisted that her plan was the only one that would work and refused to listen to Valentina's warnings.

That afternoon, Valentina was playing the piano in the living room and Maria was busy patching underwear. As Valentina fingered the piano keys, she glanced out of the window and saw something that made her blood run cold — two unpleasant-looking men were hustling Sania along toward the house. Valentina recognized immediately that they were Cheka agents of the dreaded secret police.

The men explained to Maria that Sania had been arrested in the act of passing a false ID card to Sunbatt. Just as Valentina had suspected, the People's Commissar had reported Sania's abortive deception. The Cheka agents had come with Sania to search the house.

As her mother stood hearing out the Cheka, it occurred to Valentina that she must do something about the letters they had received from her brothers and acquaintances in the White Army. After listening for a while as her mother discussed the matter with the men, she casually left them, and when she was out of the Cheka agents' line of sight, she flew up to her room. Though she tried to hurry, all she had time to do was hide the incriminating letters under the mattress in her room. She then went back and stood beside her mother, who was still talking with the men.

Valentina had a horrible premonition that the first place the Cheka agents would look when they searched her room would be under her mattress. The blood drained from Maria's face as she anticipated what fate awaited Sania. Anybody familiar with the Cheka agents' reputation could not help but be terrified. Many people had been thrown into a Cheka cell, never to be heard from again. Of course, everyone knew what happened to women who had the misfortune to fall into the hands of the Communist Party's secret police.

Valentina, however, could only think of their letters from friends and relatives and how they must not be found. If they were found, not only her mother and her sister but also Valentina herself would be thrown into prison. She would probably also be tortured to find out how the letters had reached her hands in a town under Communist Party control. The Cheka would then find out that there was a secret communications channel connecting the anti-Bolsheviks in town to the White Army and that liaison messengers were in close contact. Furthermore, they would find out that Maria had used it to keep in touch with her sons.

Valentina turned to look at her mother. Maria wore the desperate look of a mother trying to save her daughter from being carried off by two strange men. She insisted that her daughter had done what she had out of love and that it was not the sort of thing an adult should be concerned about. Furthermore, she argued that her lack of responsibility in failing to discipline her daughter implicated her, Sania's mother, as a guilty party. Sania was absolutely crushed and said not a word.

Valentina had the impression that she was the only one worried about what would happen if the letters were discovered, and she felt a bead of sweat run down her forehead. The younger of the two Cheka agents looked less daunting than the other did. Sensing that he was a good person at heart, Valentina turned to him and asked that they save time and search her room. The evil-looking one agreed to let his younger comrade search Valentina's room, and she led the way upstairs. The first thing that the agent did upon entering Valentina's room was pick up a notebook on her desk in which she had written some sentimental verses. When the young man began reading them out loud, Valentina's face reddened. The notebook was special to her and was intended for no other eyes but her own.

"Hurry up and do your job. Search the room if you please," she said in a tone of unconcern.

"The fact is that personally, I'm not the least interested in searching your room," he replied. "I'm not even a Communist Party member. I was recruited right out of high school. But it's my duty, so I'll just have a quick look around." The young man then walked toward her bed, and as he did so, Valentina's heart pounded so forcefully that she was afraid he might hear it. *If he looks under the mattress, it's all over for me,* she thought and resigned her fate to heaven. Just then the older agent came in.

"Finished with this room?" he asked.

The younger man drew himself up and replied, "Yes, I've finished."

Hearing these words, Valentina felt the tension drain out of her. The letters remained undiscovered, and the identity of the many people who had risked their lives to carry messages was kept secret.

When the house search was finished, Valentina watched the two Cheka agents lead away her sister Sania. Maria gave herself up to sobs, but she knew she could not cry forever. She had to act quickly if she were to save her daughter. She wiped away her tears and resolutely rose to her feet. She decided to get in touch with a Jewish acquaintance, who was both a Communist Party member and a high-ranking People's Commissar. She would ask him to straighten things out. This People's Commissar was a friend of Madame Simon's husband.

When Valentina woke up the next morning, Maria had already gone to visit Madame Simon. Maria had left a message not to let anyone into the house until she returned. Poor Mama! No doubt her harebrained daughter had caused her a sleepless night.

Valentina's heart felt as though it would explode with anger and fear. Why had people of the same motherland turned against each other in hatred? People with the same past and the same culture suddenly divided into executioners and victims. Who had created these cruel and horrifying ideas that under the fine pretext of the people's good had killed so many? In a world inhabited by these new ideas, there was neither beauty, nor good, nor stability. Tears ran down Valentina's cheeks as she imagined how her mother must have felt when she had left so early that morning.

Glancing throughout the window, Valentina saw a Bulgarian classmate of hers approaching, and she opened the door to let her in. Explaining everything that had happened on the previous day, she asked the girl to stay with her until her mother returned. The girl's father was a member of the working class. Also she and her family were foreigners, so she wasn't particularly frightened by what Valentina had told her.

A little while later, Valentina looked through the window and saw the older of the two agents from the day before approaching their home. There was then a knock on the door, which she felt obliged to answer.

"Aren't you going to ask me to have a seat?" asked the agent.

"No, this isn't a social visit. State your business, please," she replied with palpable scorn.

"And where is your mother?" he asked.

"I don't know."

"Where did she go?"

"I tell you I don't know. I was asleep when she went out. Look, this is the note she left me."

The agent glanced at the note but remained silent; neither did he make a move to go. Valentina seethed with rage. Unable to suppress it, she retorted, "If you haven't any business here, then leave!"

She spoke in such strong tones that both the agent and her classmate looked at her with astonishment. The agent glared for a while and considered this slip of a girl whom, if he wanted to, he could put into custody. Then, unexpectedly, he abruptly opened the door and left without saying a word.

After some time had passed, Sania came home alone. She said not a word in reply to Valentina's questions. When, at a late hour, Maria returned and saw that Sania had already been released, she wrapped her daughter in her arms and wept. That day, she had gone to ask Madame Simon to get her husband to speak on her behalf. Acting immediately, the Jewish People's Commissar arranged for Sania's release at least until the People's Trial started. The People's Commissar had offered himself as her guarantor and had asked Maria to promise that Sania wouldn't run off. The commissar warned her in the severest of terms that if Sania left town, she would be captured and immediately executed. How could she escape when she had nowhere to go? And in those times, who would dare hide her anyway? If someone did, they would be held equally culpable. Such were Maria's thoughts in the face of the commissar's dire warnings.

For the purpose of keeping them under surveillance, a new People's Commissar was billeted in their house. He wasn't a bad person, but in the evening, his many friends and drinking buddies would gather in the living room. On these occasions, Maria and her daughters kept to their rooms with their doors shut tightly because one could never know what a drunken man would do. These men would drink until dawn, and sometimes Maria discovered one man or another sleeping on the dining table, wrapped in one of the immaculate white tablecloth. The female friends of the party members who attended the drinking parties helped themselves to the closets full of luxurious clothing, bedding, tablecloths, and tableware left behind by the merchant owner. Perfume and expensive underwear met with the same fate.

The war was still going on. A force of forty-five thousand former Czech prisoners of war who had joined up with the White Army to fight the Bolsheviks was nearing Ekaterinburg, where the abdicated Nicholas and his family were now confined. The lengthy process of a people's court was considered no longer feasible, and on July 16, 1918, Lenin personally ordered the Soviet Government of the Ural Administrative Division to shoot Nicholas and his whole family.

A mere eight days after the assassination of the Romanovs the joint Czech and White Army force retook Ekaterinburg, Matushka Maria, who had been brought up in the town of Perm, also in the Urals and not far from Ekaterinburg, was stunned speechless by the horrific news. Twenty-one years earlier, Maria and her husband had been granted an audience with the young Tsar Nicholas at St. Nicholas Church, where Father Valerian officiated, and she remembered the day as if it were yesterday. Nicholas's four beautiful daughters chanced to be almost the same ages as her own four children, making the sad news even more painful for her to bear.

Sobbing with grief, Maria crossed herself and prayed for the souls of the tsar and his family.

The Borotinski family was forced to live under Red Army occupation. Under Communist rule, Russian people were required to submit docilely, like sheep, to the new Communist teachings, but they also had to believe in their Communist leaders and revere them as if they were gods. For the Russian citizens, daily life was filled with fear of regime mixed with a dull, lifeless boredom.

The Bolsheviks were determined to oppress religion. They destroyed all the churches in a supreme atheist Bolshevik aim of uprooting religion from the minds of the people. They persecuted the clergy and pious believers and severely repressed the activities of the antirevolutionary and imperial restoration movements. Ekaterinodar, under Red Army occupation, was no exception.

Sania's day in People's Court was fast approaching. Maria was worried; she could not sleep. What could she expect of this rough-hewn crew of drunkards called the Red Army? The situation looked hopeless, and Maria prayed devotedly to God. Then one day, Father Valerian, her pillar of strength, returned from the distant church where he had been assisting the priest who was ill.

It was now the day before the trial. The People's Commissar who had been detailed to keep watch over them returned to Maria's house. He looked out of temper. He announced to Maria that sudden business required him to leave town for a while.

Maria had heard that the White Army was closing on Ekaterinodar. Indeed, the sound of artillery and rifle fire could now be heard drawing ever nearer. The White Army had once before come close to relieving the city, but at the last moment, they had retreated, and so Ekaterinodar residents could not rest easy. Maria and the others had little confidence that the White Army could so easily retake the town.

Valentina sensed the change in the mood of the commissar who was staying at the Borotinski house. When Valentina was a young girl, she had often gone to Gatchina to visit Tantochka, and by watching her aunt, she had learned how to tell fortunes with a deck of cards. Although she hadn't learned how to do it in any proper way, the commissar staying with them would sometimes ask her to do a reading for him. On this day, the commissar had come back with a bleak look on his face. Valentina, in response to his unusually grave request, agreed to do a reading for him. While pretending to tell his fortune, Valentina had been able to ask him a number of questions, and she gradually came to understand what it was that caused him such concern. It was her hunch that with the approach of the White Army, the commissar was afraid he might be captured. So she hinted that a tragic event awaited him in the near future. Heaving a great sigh, he asked question after question about his future.

Completely taken in by her reading, the commissar immediately set about packing. Although her heart was singing, Valentina wore a serious face as she helped the commissar to pack. Some people standing in the garden saw her come out of the house behind the commissar, who was now carrying a suitcase. Turning toward them, Valentina gave them a playful smirk, and the people stared at her in amazement, unable to comprehend what was happening.

On the day that Sania was to appear in People's Court, the Red Army was in no position to mount a trial because the White Army was approaching fast. In the afternoon, artillery shells whistled over the town. Everyone knew that the gunfire came from the White Army, so no one was afraid. When night fell, the tempo of artillery fire quickened. The atmosphere was very tense.

That night, most of the people in the town stayed awake. Valentina's mother had to tell her repeatedly not to sit by the window, but Valentina wouldn't listen. From her window, Valentina saw something that she never imagined she would ever see. Late that night, as Valentina entered her second-floor bedroom, she heard a very strange noise and looked out of her window. The night was lit by a full moon, and Valentina could see the street very clearly from where she stood. There, some distance away on the road that passed by her house, she beheld a scene that was as strangely beautiful as it was horrifying—a battle between two detachments of mounted Cossacks, the Reds against the Whites, Cossack brother against Cossack brother.

Illumined by the soft moonlight, the two cavalry detachments fought with each other, their Cossack sabers glinting. Strangely, there were no shouts. All Valentina could hear were the sounds of metal against metal, frightened noises of horses, and occasionally an "Ahhh," like a groan, as a Cossack, mortally wounded, slid off his saddle and fell onto the snow-covered ground. Valentina, who had never before seen a man die, almost fainted. This scene of fratricidal carnage became etched deep into her memory forever, and years later, she spoke of it often to her children.

People from the neighborhood slowly gathered at Valentina's house and huddled on the veranda, where they sat noiselessly in the dark. Everyone trembled with fear. Rumor held that the Communists were waiting to ambush them with machine guns when they came out to greet the White Army. No one knew how reliable the talk was, but by the same token, nobody wanted to risk doing anything dangerous. An eerie silence descended over the town, as if it were empty of people. Something was about to happen, but no one knew quite what. Suddenly, there came a knock at the gate, and they all looked at each other. Father Valerian left to see who was there. Valerian had not yet returned when a group of Cossacks in black uniforms entered the garden and walked over to where the neighbors were gathered on the veranda. The Cossacks all wore white scarves around their caps to signify that they were White Army men, but no one dared trust that it was so. The Cossacks just stood there without saying a word.

Then an old woman from the neighborhood ran out into the garden, crying, "Mishenka, Mishenka!" and wrapped her arms around a young Cossack. Turning to the people on the veranda, she announced, "It's all right. Don't be scared. They're the real thing—genuine White Army. This is my youngest boy Mishenka!"

There was an uproar as everyone hugged and kissed each other with joy. Maria and the others urged the Cossack officers to take off their coats and put down their weapons. They asked question after question as they did so. Maria then laid out for them every morsel of food and every drop of drink available. They learned from the men that the main force of the White Army was still fighting to reach the town. The Reds were slowly retreating. Their own unit had been given the mission of reconnoitering the town in order to secure a place that could serve as a headquarters building.

This White Army unit decided that Maria's big house was perfectly suited for a headquarters. The reconnaissance party left after telling them to ready the house for the White Army that would soon arrive.

CHAPTER 16

Valentina Elopes

On August 15, 1918, the White Army marched triumphantly into Ekaterinodar, and every flower bed worthy of the name surrendered its blossoms to the conquering heroes. Valentina, now sixteen, went out into the streets with her mother and sister to hail the victors. They spotted an old friend of Nicholas among the vanguard and wasted no time in asking after his safety.

"Not a scratch!" they were assured. "He'll be along any minute now." And sure enough, there he was, astride an artillery tank, grinning from ear to ear. Ecstatic with joy, they ran to him, arms outstretched, and each embraced a part of him.

The town burst with excitement. Everyone imagined that this day marked the beginning of a grand new era of White Army victories.

Soon Modest and Olga would join them. Valerian would be able to visit, and finally Maria's sons would be nearby when she needed them. No longer would the Borotinski women have to fend for themselves. Under the Reds—in the long months before the White Army retook the town—there had been countless arrests, courts-martial, and executions, leaving a legacy of dread that hung like a pall over the town.

Maria and her daughters could now go back to the uneventful but blissfully normal way of life they had led in the past.

As Valentina and her sister watched the seemingly endless procession of triumphant White soldiers, Sania suddenly let out a shout. Valentina turned and saw the Cheka agent who had arrested Sania astride a White Army horse, his face now masked in a jubilant smile. Sania and Valentina pointed at the horse rider and called out, "Oh no! That's a Red Army spy!" Nicholas and his friend, a White Army major, elbowed their way through the crowd, pulled the man down from his horse, and had him arrested and taken to White Army headquarters.

This was not the only unusual occurrence to mark that day. After Nicholas and his comrades settled in at Maria's house and were enjoying the feast the women had prepared for them, Sunbatt, the Circassian with whom Sania had fallen in love, appeared and announced that he was going to have Sania arrested for putting his life in danger during the Red Army occupation. What a thing to have happened on this most joyous of days! Fortunately, Nicholas and his friends stepped in and smoothed the matter over. What a relief it was to have a few men in the house when things threatened to get out of hand!

However, the civil war was not over yet. Although the Red Army had retreated and the Whites were on the offensive, the fighting still continued. Trainloads of sick and wounded arrived daily from the front, filling the hospital. There was neither sufficient staff nor adequate medical supplies, and the place was little better than a field hospital. So it was that Sania, a trained nurse, received a warm welcome at the hospital. Valentina volunteered her services, as well, after school.

Her chief occupations were making bandages from rags and assisting the nurses. Without complaint, she devoted herself to the care of soldiers, some of whom she saw languish and die of illness or wounds before her very eyes.

On June 4, 1918, Valentina graduated from Ekaterinodar Women's School. With the exception of mathematics, her only weak subject in which she earned a C, Valentina received straight As. Hoping to put her best field of study to use by becoming a teacher of foreign languages, Valentina set about earning a teacher's license. To qualify, it was necessary for her to take a special training course lasting an additional year.

Over the summer, until school began in September, Valentina devoted herself heart and soul to service at the hospital. There was a very handsome young officer among the soldiers who were sent back from the front for medical treatment. Unlike so many of the others, he never moaned or cried out in pain when his bandages were changed. She learned from the nurse who looked after him that he was an infantry captain named Aleksei Zhukov. Because of his multiple wounds, he had been offered preferment to a position in the rear of the troops, but he had declined, saying that there were plenty of reservists to fill such posts. His return to the front was of his own choosing. The nurse who had shared this information with Valentina was a woman in her twenties, who was obviously attracted to Captain Zhukov.

One day, during the final stage of his recovery, the captain dressed himself to go for a walk. Seeing him in uniform for the first time, Valentina stood breathless. She couldn't take her eyes off his gallant figure. He wore the splendid dress uniform of the White Army with six gold stripes on the sleeves. Perhaps because he had noticed her staring at him, her cheeks flushed. The captain smiled and casually asked her to join him for a walk through town and a meal at a restaurant later.

Valentina's heart raced at this unexpected invitation. Until now, her male friends had all been students her own age, and none had ever asked her to share a meal with them at a restaurant. She was ecstatic. It seemed that for the first time in her life, she was being treated like a woman. In the course of their conversation over lunch, her affinity toward him was further strengthened when she learned that the captain was her brother Nicholas's commanding officer. After their meal, the two walked in the park. By the time she reached home, her heart belonged to the captain, and Valentina now set about hatching a plan to wrest him from his nurse, who in short order had become her rival whose transparent infatuation concerned her.

Among the few pieces of jewelry that Maria had brought from the capital was a sapphire ring that Valentina rarely saw her mother wear. She put the ring on the ring finger of her right hand before setting out the next day for the hospital. Though she intended her rival to take notice, it was essential that Valentina maintain an air of nonchalance. Her rival, however, took immediate note of the bauble and asked if Valentina was planning to get married.

"Well, as a matter of fact...," Valentina said and hesitated, as if it were a great secret, before saying, "Don't tell a soul but..."

When the nurse heard that the man was none other than her patient, Captain Zhukov, she dashed off in distress to the captain's ward and took him to task for not informing her of his engagement to Valentina. The captain was momentarily taken aback, but he chose not to deny it.

The next day, Captain Zhukov again invited Valentina to have lunch with him, and as they ate, the two laughed impishly over their make-believe marriage. They decided to maintain, for the time being, the fiction that they were about to marry, and the news spread quickly through every ward of the hospital. The whole hospital bubbled with excitement over the coming marriage of the manly captain to the innocent young nurse's aide. However, the colonel who commanded Captain Zhukov's brigade, and whose permission to wed he was obliged to seek, stopped Valentina one day in the corridor and asked her why, if the captain's intentions were indeed honorable, he had not informed the colonel of them.

Valentina was shocked to learn that what she had intended as no more than a jealous little joke had now gotten completely out of hand. She confessed all to the colonel, even telling him that the ring she had represented as her engagement ring actually belonged to her mother. In the course of that day, she returned the ring to her mother's jewelry box and vowed never to engage in such tomfoolery again. For his part, the colonel ordered Captain Zhukov to appear before him and strictly censured him for participating in this bit of silliness that might have reflected on the honor of a young unmarried woman.

The next day, worried over what had passed between the two officers, Valentina sought the company of the captain. He invited her to have lunch with him once again, and without any prompting at all from her, he told her what he had said to his commanding officer.

"What began as a playful charade," he said, "became my heart's desire. If that girl feels as I do, then in jest is truth."

The captain seemed to be making a genuine proposal of marriage. Valentina's heart beat madly, and she felt as nervous as a mouse beset by a cat. Her confusion was so great that she could hardly speak. "But . . . Mother and Father and my brothers too . . ." The words stuck in her throat. The captain, a smile playing at the corners of his lips, continued her list of family inventory. "Oh yes, and your sister, your grandmother, and your grandfather too. What will they all say?"

Valentina's consternation aroused by his proposal was exactly as the captain had imagined it would be. Maria put her foot down as soon as Valentina broached the subject. Maria was not going to sit by and watch her daughter get married to a soldier who had been wounded any number of times she said. To begin with, the captain was all of twelve years older than her daughter. Furthermore, other than the fact that his father was a railway stationmaster in Lithuania, Maria knew nothing of the captain's family, and she thought it likely that he had an unsavory past. Certainly he was fine to look at, but Maria felt something cold in him.

The more vociferously her mother voiced her opposition, the more worthy did her captain appear to Valentina. Turning a deaf ear to her parents, she met secretly with Captain Zhukov. This did not last for long, since his wounds finally healed and the time approached for him to return to the battlefield. After the captain left, Valentina continued with her language course and wrote to him one letter every day.

Winter came. There was a major engagement with the Red Army, and most of the sick and wounded came to Ekaterinodar. Among them was Captain Zhukov. This time he had taken a bullet, which had lodged deep in his lung. Nurses with experience of such cases warned Valentina that chest wounds were inevitably complicated with tuberculosis. When she realized that the man she loved was in such a grave condition, she no longer listened to her parents. Nothing could be so disloyal, Valentina felt, than a woman who dissolved her engagement because her fiancé was in poor health.

Valentina's parents' opposition was no match for the obstinacy and single-minded devotion of their daughter. To the horror of Father Valerian and Matushka Maria, Valentina decided to elope with Captain Zhukov. As the daughter of a priest, however, Valentina wanted a formal blessing and marriage in the church by a priest. The young couple went to the village priest and asked him to marry them. The priest agreed but required the bride and bridegroom to go to confession before the ceremony. Valentina noted with surprise that Aleksei's confession was an amazingly long one. The wedding ceremony consisting only of the bride and bridegroom took place in a little church in Ekaterinodar on an April day in 1919. On May 15, the seventeen-year-old Valentina completed her course as a married woman in language studies with excellent grades, thus earning her license to teach Russian.

CHAPTER 17

Kharkov

It was a honeymoon amid civil war, yet Valentina was happy. Captain Aleksei Zhukov was commander of the artillery car of an armored railway train called "Slava Ofitseru" (Glory to the officer). At the beginning of their marriage, Aleksei would journey from his post to visit his bride, but he soon came to realize that it would be much more convenient if she came to the town where his armored train was based. Having thus made the decision, they rented a room in the home of a wealthy widow where Valentina waited longingly and impatiently for word from her husband telling her to set out. At this time, Aleksei would send his pay home from the front, a fairly large sum of money in those days. In the lush garden in the wealthy woman's yard, there stood a small sauna-type bathhouse that was completely surrounded by greenery. The bathhouse was covered with grapevines and lilacs, and it was here that Valentina stayed as she awaited word from her husband. Rumors flew about the army falling apart. Deserters roamed around looking for an easy gain. Even in the Cossack stations, instances of hooliganism had begun to occur.

One night, having received the pay from her husband earlier that day, Valentina suffered an unpleasant incident. Valentina was about to fall asleep when a dog began to bark at the top of its voice. The dog did not have an owner and spent all its time under the bathhouse window. It was a moonlit night, and there was no curtain on the window. Valentina turned off the light and looked out of the window. A Cossack with a gun in his hand was circling the house, but the dog's growling and barking viciously was preventing the Cossack from coming near the house. Valentina could see that the man was trying to scare the dog off with the butt of his rifle. Valentina had no weapons whatsoever, except for a small grenade without the charger. The bathhouse had only one door, and the windows were too small to allow for crawling through. The bathhouse turned out to be a mousetrap! Valentina grabbed the useless grenade and jumped out of the bathhouse with the shout "I shall shoot!" The Cossack, believing that Valentina had a revolver, fled as fast as he could. After that night, Valentina's life became unbearable. She was afraid of sleeping in the bathhouse and moved in with Matushka Maria and Modest's wife, Olga.

Olga had given birth to a son and was now living with Matushka Maria. Modest served as an officer under Aleksei. The armored train was based at Kharkov in Ukraine, some 500 kilometers north of Ekaterinodar, but to get there by train one had to connect at Rostov-on-Don. Valentina and Aleksei had agreed that he would rent a room for her in Kharkov so that they could be together when the armored train returned from the front lines.

But no letter arrived from Aleksei. *It is possible that Aleksei's letter had gotten lost along the way*, Valentina thought. Unable to wait any longer and driven by a consuming desire to be with her husband, Valentina decided to go on her own to Kharkov. She knew the name of the hotel where Aleksei stayed when he was in Kharkov, and that was surely enough to reach him. Having made up her mind, she went directly to the bank to withdraw money to buy the things she would need for her trip. *In the event that Aleksei himself comes to the station to fetch me, I would also have to look presentable for him*, she reasoned. In her heart, she was already safe and sound in Aleksei's arms in Kharkov.

If the war would only go away and leave her to be with her husband, she pined, they could finally be happy. Many were the hours they had spent planning the things that they would do and the sort of house they would live in. As long as the war continued, every precious hour together was viewed as a gift from on high.

By now, the 1919 winter had set in, and Valentina worried about taking the long journey alone.

Valentina learned from her sister that an officer she had met at the hospital was leaving for Kharkov on the same day she herself planned to leave. Valentina and the officer arranged that he should collect Valentina's luggage packed with all her possessions, including most of the money she had received from Aleksei, and carry it to the station. However, on the appointed day, the departure time came and went, but no officer appeared.

All Valentina had in her possession were a few rubles in her purse and the conviction that if she could just get to Kharkov, Aleksei would straighten everything out. The station at Rostov-on-Don was thronged, and changing trains for Kharkov was a touch-and-go affair. In many railway stations, there were huge icons of Saint Nicholas, protector of travelers. Valentina looked and found herself in front of one such icon. She sat on a bench and firmly awaited the train, all the while praying and sucking juice from a lemon. She was not even praying with words but was merely looking at the icon with the hope that help would come. Suddenly, Valentina saw Alfred, the son of her French teacher, Madame Simon. He was headed in the opposite direction. Alfred was a Russian citizen and so was mobilized by the White Army to fight. Valentina's own brothers had helped him to board the armored train. However, Alfred did not get along with anyone there, and there was real danger of his being sent to an infantry unit. He was now on his way to visit his father in Novorossiysk. Both Alfred and Valentina were cold and hungry. Alfred managed to sell his silver cigarette lighter, and with this money, they bought a good dinner and a ticket for Valentina. The following morning, Alfred left, and Valentina continued to wait as before. Valentina sat facing the icon of St. Nicholas, silently praying for a miracle. It was terribly cold. When the train pulled in, the platform was covered in snow, and it was so frozen that Valentina's footsteps made crunching sounds as though she were walking on sugar. Somehow, Valentina managed to get aboard one of several military trains to which civilian carriages had been coupled.

A soldier she met on the train treated her kindly and took it upon himself to see her safely to Kharkov. He was an army pharmacist named Leonid, who had contracted typhus at the hospital where he had been posted. Now recovered, he was headed home on leave to Kharkov.

Valentina told him about her misfortune and how she had ended up in Rostov-on-Don. Valentina learned much about the war situation from this soldier, but the news that stunned her most was that the White Army, having suffered many casualties, was not up to strength and was now forced to fall back to Kharkov, which it was ordered to defend at all cost.

Valentina would have to return, but the only clothes she had were those she wore, and the little money in her purse wouldn't even buy her a return ticket. She did not know what to do.

Leonid felt pity for the woman and, calling her Little Sister, arranged for the two of them to travel in one of the cars reserved for troops. From the moment their train pulled out of Ekaterinodar station, everything went wrong. Cold and exhausted, she borrowed a soldier's greatcoat hanging on a hook by the window and wrapped herself in it. Once she had warmed herself, she dozed off to sleep. During this trip, Valentina had nothing to eat. Leonid was unable to go and fetch bread. They drank water from a dirty bottle, which Leonid begged from drunken soldiers.

Finally, the train drew close to Kharkov. The train was going through the Izjumski Forest. It was cold, gray, and damp.

When Valentina awoke, dawn was breaking as the train moved slowly through a forest covered white with snow. Kharkov seemed so close. Suddenly, the train stopped and the soldiers prepared to get off. What were the soldiers going to do? Were they going for a breath of fresh air and a stretch? A very disturbing announcement was made that the train could not proceed to Kharkov because the Red Army had damaged the rails in front of them. All passengers would have to get off at this point and walk the rest of the way to Kharkov with their luggage.

Valentina was just about to stand up and obey the announcement, when Leonid stopped her from doing so. "Do not move," he whispered. "I could not sleep last night, and I overheard what they were planning to do . . ."

After a half hour, they heard shooting in the forest.

"Red Army?" asked Valentina.

"No, it is not," answered Leonid. "Just pretend to be asleep," answered Leonid.

Valentina was now wide awake. Making a small hole in the army coat that covered her, she peeked through the window. Through her tiny peephole, she saw soldiers coming back from the woods carrying many pieces of luggage. *So the shots I had heard were of the soldiers who had just murdered the civilian passengers for their baggage?* It seemed also that many soldiers had not returned to the train but had disappeared into the forest. Deserters? Is this how the army conducted itself? Having witnessed such shameful and criminal acts committed by the soldiers, Valentina shook with fear and disgust.

Despite the announcement that it was not going to Kharkov, the train suddenly started moving forward and, in a half hour, it arrived at Kharkov. The train was twenty-four hours late. Aleksei had not known that his wife would arrive on it. Leonid kindly asked the station master where Aleksei's armored train was. The latter replied that he had been told it had just left from another Kharkov train station for the battle somewhere. Leonid suggested Valentina to stay at his parents' home until the armored train had come back.

At that moment, Valentina made a decision unbeknownst to her, which proved to be momentous. Had she taken Leonid's advice to wait for the return of the armored train, Valentina would have been forever stuck in Russia; it was December 1919.

Instead, Valentina took a streetcar towards the direction of Balashov railway station where the armored train had previously stopped. The streetcar brought Valentina up to a bridge near the station. It did not cross the bridge for fear the bridge might be mined. Valentina however, had a premonition that Aleksei was still in Kharkov. She decided to go and see where Aleksei's army train was supposed to be. It was snowing, and Valentina was hungry and tired. Further, she could no longer walk. Finally, she sat down on a pile of snow and prayed silently, half-conscious. She heard shooting from within the town; at times, the shooting drew nearer and then moved farther away. Leaning against the railing of the bridge in desperation, she fervently prayed to Saint Nicholas for his help. Meanwhile, people were passing hurriedly by her. The sound of heavy gunfire echoed from the other end of the city. People were obviously rushing home before the fighting reached them. No one took notice of the young woman desperately praying on the bridge. One such passing person, an officer, however, slowed down to take a closer look at her. For a while, he hesitated but then ran toward her.

"Valya! You! What on God's earth are you doing here?"

Valentina looked up.

"Alyosha!"

It was a miracle! Her own husband was standing in front of her, but her vision was getting blurred. Raising her up gently, Aleksei said, "We have only thirty minutes before our train leaves. I was just on my way to my hotel room to pick up the luggage."

However, seeing his wife in such condition, exhausted, hungry, and sick, Aleksei decided to forget about retrieving his luggage from his hotel. Instead, he hailed a coach to take them to the station where his armored train was waiting. He even had to threaten the driver with his pistol to take them, since all the coach-drivers were rushing home to their families before the town changed hands and became occupied by the Red Army. The Whites were leaving Kharkov.

From this time on, Valentina traveled as a passenger on the train on which her husband was a gunnery officer. His armored train "Slava ofitseru" (Glory to the officer) had been based at Kharkov. Her two brothers, Modest and Nicholas, were also in the same train. Hearing that their sister was in the train, they came to see her. They took turns shouting at her.

"For heaven's sake, have you gone crazy? What were you thinking to have come to such a dangerous place all alone?"

However, other officers were impressed by her bravery. They even gave her some gifts which they had bought at the railway station. Valentina lay on a seat in a Pullman car. She was feverish and hungry but very happy.

Aleksei let his wife stay in his compartment. In no time, the train left Kharkov for South Rostov. Aleksei ordered a soldier to bring a uniform and told Valentina, "There is a rule that we cannot have civilians on the armored train. You must wear this and pretend you are a soldier."

He then took her, clad in baggy military garb, to the artillery car, which he explained was the safest place on the train. When Aleksei introduced his wife to his subordinates, they turned to look at her in amazement and studied with the greatest curiosity their commander's young wife, who had made her way alone into the maelstrom of war to battle at her husband's side.

APPENDIX

Photos & Graphics

Grandfather Fedot Ivanovich Borotinski

Father Valerian Fedotovich Borotinski

Mother Maria Kapitonovna Borotinski

Valentina Borotinski

Husband Aleksei Zhukov

Sister-in-law Olga Borotinski

Borotinski family in Skopje

Father Valerian & Matushka Maria

Girl's High School in Split 1935 —
Valentina's Homeroom

Split 1937 — Valentina and Vladimir

Kamnik, Slovenia, 1947 — Valentina and Anatole

Toronto, Canada, 1964 —
Vladimir, Emiko, Anatole, Valentina

Toronto 1954: With son Boris

Honolulu, 1974

Honolulu, 1984. Valentina and Emiko

Honolulu, 1986: Nicholas, Valentina, and Andrei

Honolulu, 1994:
Nicholas, baby Valentina and Alyona

Father Anatole and Matushka Emiko
on a Pilgrimage in Jerusalem, 2009.

Great-Granddaughter Valentina, 2012

CHAPTER 18

Amidst Civil War

As the artillery train made its way across the war-torn landscape, it met with frequent fire from enemy ambushes. During these attacks, the customarily cheerful troops were courageous and serious in front of Valentina as they fired round after round of artillery at the Reds. When the train advanced unopposed, however, Valentina was surprised to see this other side of the troopers, who gaily sang Russian folk songs or told hilarious jokes in the effort to make their commander's young wife laugh. The soldiers were very fond of her husband. They appreciated his bravery and fairness.

The train stopped for several days at a station along the way to refuel and undergo repairs, and during this pause, Aleksei and Valentina finally found the opportunity to talk and tell each other all the things they had been keeping until they could finally meet again. She learned from Aleksei that he had written to her, advising her not to come because of the deteriorating strength of the White Army and the possibility of Kharkov falling into enemy hands. The fact that his letter had not reached her testified to the frailty of communications.

"Because of the civil war, we have lost the war with our foreign enemy," he said, spitting out the words. "While two dogs fought over a bone, a third made off with it."

Repairs to the train were soon completed, and once again, they set out for Rostov-on-Don. Because the territory they would be entering was very dangerous, Aleksei told Valentina to go back and stay with Maria and Anastasia. But Valentina couldn't bear the thought of leaving her husband and brothers and begged to stay just a little longer.

It was Christmastime, and at one of the rest stops, someone decided they should have a little celebration, even in the midst of a civil war. The soldiers brought in a tree from outside. The passengers decorated the branches of the tree with shreds of colored paper, candies, and even walnuts. In the officers' dining car, they even managed to prepare a sumptuous dinner, but even amidst the celebrations, everyone remained fully aware that the festivities would be short-lived and that this respite from fighting was only temporary.

The end of the celebration came with an explosion on another train stationed near them. Nobody knew the reason for the explosion. Some soldiers conjectured that perhaps careless smoking had ignited some ammunition. In the darkness between explosions, Valentina could discern the figures of brave individuals earnestly working to detach those railway cars which had not caught fire. Their bravery saved the passenger cars, and the passengers were spared from being kicked out onto the snow-covered platform of the railway station. But the train could not leave. Their locomotive departed with the battlewagons, and there was not a spare locomotive in sight. But they were saved by the grace of God when the soldiers succeeded in detaching the burning cars, and the explosions finally ceased. Advance scouts returned to report that in Rostov-on-Don, their destination, local Cossacks who had joined the Bolsheviks had taken power and had cut off the way to Novorossiysk.

Before the trains could go very far, a reconnaissance vehicle brought them the news that the Reds lay in ambush further down the tracks and that the situation in the Rostov region had deteriorated into mob rule. Aleksei's armored train had decided that they should abandon the train, cross the frozen Don River, and link up with a contingent of White Army soldiers retreating from Rostov. However, the initial plan was to try to fight their way through. This would be accomplished by the sudden appearance in Rostov railway station of six compositions of armored trains. The women and several wounded would be sent by oxcarts around the city along the railway line. Passenger cars would then be burned later. However, this decision was later rejected as being very unwise. It was made in haste. If armored trains were blocked from further progress, then any railway cars carrying women and wounded had no chance of crossing the danger zone. Someone commandeered some horses and carriages. These were used for hauling the wounded and weaker women. Valentina was given a horse. She donned whatever warm clothing she could find.

It was a bitterly cold night when the caravan began its journey. Astride the horse, Valentina followed the procession. The column marched on in silence.

A bright moon enfolded the night in an unearthly hush. As far as the eye could see, the steppes extended under a blanket of snow. Valentina forgot for a while the ravages of war and recalled the happy years she had spent as a child in St. Petersburg. She wondered about her uncles, her cousins, and her classmates—those she had left behind in St. Petersburg.

Would she never again see them? How swiftly had the world of human affairs changed! Amidst its constant cycle of change, the natural world seemed unchanging and ever so beautiful.

In the sky above, the thousands of luminous stars sparkled like gems. Suddenly, Valentina realized she was all alone. She must have dozed off. Around her, the snowfields stretched on endlessly in the moonlight. Where had everyone gone? She could not see a living creature in sight, and she was terrified. She rode on until she was approached by a unit of Cossacks. A man who seemed to be in command spoke, "If you don't want to fall into the hands of the Reds," he said, "come with us."

At this, one of the soldiers dismounted and pointed to tracks in the snow. "It looks like the people she's with went that way!"

The man who seemed to be their leader spoke again, "In that case, send her off in their tracks! Unless, of course, she wants to come with us!"

Valentina thanked them and followed the tracks in the snow into a wood. Soon enough, and not too far away, she caught up with Aleksei, who had been searching frantically for her. His look of utter despair turned to relief when he looked and saw her. "Where in the world did you learn to sleep on horseback?" he asked, and he took her horse by the reins.

"This place is crawling with Red Army troops," he told her. "We've got to get back to the column right now. There's still a good chance we'll get through. When we fall in with the White Army, I want you to go back to your parents. Don't worry about me. As long as I draw breath, I'll never leave you. Someday, somewhere, we'll have a life together."

It took the caravan one day and night to cross about 40 miles. They had to cross the frozen Don River covered with snow and ice. From time to time, the exhausted Valentina needed to stop and rest. She would find a place on a snow bank, then would refuse to continue marching with the others. Finally, the soldiers were able to commandeer some oxcarts, which they loaded with machine guns and ammunition. On top of this, they put Valentina along with the sergeant nicknamed Chizhik (Little Finch), who was there to see that Valentina would not fall off. However, in spite of Chizhik, Valentina fell off the cart, on her belly, flat on the ice, in front of the cart! Luckily, the soldiers walking beside the cart managed to grab the wheels and prevent the cart from moving and running over her until Valentina could be pulled back up. And so, back on top of the cart, Valentina continued her journey.

The sick and the wounded had to be dragged along the ice in blankets. There were no stretchers. Their nourishment consisted of snow and dried herrings, which they tore into and ate with their bare hands.

In this manner, they reached another branch of the railway line, which turned out to be still in White hands and relatively unthreatened. It also happened that a White armored train, *Iva Kalita*, was on that line. This train had been nicknamed the Ivan Cain because it was well known for shirking combat. It seems that the main preoccupation of this train's commander and crew was to forage for good food supplies. That is why this train happened to be on a relatively safe branch of the railway line.

The *Ivan Cain* transported women and the wounded away from the front and connected with a passenger train that would take them to safety.

The train commander decided that it was now too dangerous even for his wife Lida to stay back with him. Since she would be going in the same direction, Lida agreed to accompany Valentina home.

The two women, separated from their husbands, shared their fears that the White Army was doomed and that victory was now forever out of reach. They decided to rest at a hotel until the time came for their train to leave. How many days had it been since they had slept comfortably in a bed! Exhausted, the two soon fell asleep.

The next morning, Valentina didn't feel well. She had never before felt such nausea. Lida immediately realized that Valentina was pregnant and had her examined by the local doctor, who verified that she was three months along.

Looking haggard and pale, Valentina arrived at her parents' door in the Cossack village, where they had sought refuge after leaving Ekaterinodar. Maria immediately sensed her daughter's condition. For several days, Valentina remained in bed.

Sometime before Valentina's arrival, her sister-in-law Olga had given birth to Modest's son Dmitry, and every morning she went with the boy for a walk. In the park and along the streets, she gathered bits of information. From what she learned, it seemed that the Red Army was drawing near and in a few days' time was likely to occupy the village.

Father Valerian, Maria, Olga, and Valentina held a family meeting and resolved unanimously to flee to the Black Sea port town of Novorossiysk. Russia's erstwhile ally, England, maintained a refugee facility there. That night, quite unexpectedly, Modest appeared. He had been ordered by his fellow White Army officer and brother-in-law Captain Aleksei Zhukov to take leave and get in contact with their family. Besides the unhappy news that the White Army was on the run, he brought a letter from Captain Zhukov for Valentina, which was as follows:

My Beloved Valya,

I don't have time to tell you how much I love you. Don't wait for me, but pack your things and go with the family to Novorossiysk to apply for an exit visa. Don't worry about me. No matter where you go, whether it's to the ends of the earth, I will find you. Be well and take care of yourself.

With love, and forever yours,
Alyosha

CHAPTER 19

Novorossiysk

It had taken Modest all day to get home, and he was so exhausted he could hardly speak. He slept soundly into the next day and rose around noon. He then described in greater detail how grave the situation was for the White Army.

"The Bolsheviks are moving at great speed," he said to the family. "In two to three days, they will have reached this station. Our Army is losing the war. The Cossacks are deserting the front lines and flocking back to their villages. They are negotiating with the Red Army for Cossack independence from Russia. The Red Army is promising anything and everything to everybody. In short, pack your things and try not to attract notice as you make your way to Novorossiysk. White Army headquarters has arranged for a special train so that the families can still get there safely. It's still possible to get out through Novorossiysk.

"Father, would you please find a Cossack you can trust and ask him to bring two wagons and horses and get everyone safely to the station under cover of night?" said Modest. "Nicholas, Aleksei, and I will remain in Mother Russia to fight the Communists."

As they listened to Modest's report, Matushka Maria and Olga were reduced to tears by the heartbreaking inevitability of what until then had been merely a possibility that they might have to leave their motherland. The pregnant Valentina stared off into the mid-distance, listening but not moving a muscle.

Only Father Valerian listened without losing his calm. When Modest finished speaking, Valerian quietly said, "It seems the Lord has made up his mind what we must do. I'll ask for horses and wagons at church tomorrow. When would be a good time to leave?"

The next evening, a pair of wagons quietly left the village amidst cold winds and flurries of snowflakes. Neither the creatures who pulled the wagons nor those who rode made a sound. Most of the windows of the houses they passed were dark. A few flickered with pale lamplight. In such a still, calm scene it seemed that nothing in the world could be amiss. When they reached the station, Valerian thanked the drivers and made a move to pay them. One of the Cossacks refused the offer of money and said, "Pray for those of us who remain at home, Father." The other took the money and left without a word.

At the station, a cluster of people waited for the White Army train that was to arrive. Several young mothers carried babies wrapped in blankets. Little children clung to their mothers' skirts. Valentina noticed a few elderly people as well. The Borotinskis joined the group.

At length, the train for Novorossiysk arrived. The lights in the cars had been extinguished, and it was pitch-dark inside. An officer who stepped down from the train saluted Modest and guided the Borotinskis to their seats, helping them with their baggage. Modest embraced his wife (in whose arms nestled his child), his parents, and then his sister Valentina. He offered a prayer for their well-being and said farewell. They watched him walk away, each holding precious thoughts for him locked in their hearts.

Valentina was jolted awake as the train hurtled into the dark night. Looking around she saw that her parents, her sister-in-law Olga, and even her little nephew were all sleeping peacefully. She felt an inexpressible sadness and outrage rise within her from being compelled to leave the country of her birth under such circumstances. Whose fault was this? To what end was this bloody civil war being fought? The Great War had ended in November 1918, so why must Russia keep on fighting? It filled her with an immense anger. Eventually, however, lulled by the monotonous swaying of the train, she fell asleep once more.

The port town of Novorossiysk, situated on the eastern shore of the Black Sea, was known for such strong northeasterly winds that they were said to overturn carriages and even, on occasion, derail a train. Novorossiysk, city of winds, was also a major terminus for trains from every quarter, and it was the only port from which White Army families, their sick and wounded, and refugees could emigrate. General G. F. Milne, Commander of Allied Occupation Forces in Constantinople, had directed that refugees of Britain's ally Russia be provided with assistance. Similarly, France and Belgium, also allies of Russia, transported refugees out of Novorossiysk.

It was a cold winter day in December 1919 when the Borotinskis arrived in this town, swollen with desperate soldiers and refugees from all parts of Russia. The Borotinski family could find no place to sleep, even for a nap. The British immigration officials stood ready to handle the registration of refugees seeking to emigrate, but the Borotinskis decided to put off applying for emigration until they had contacted their sons and son-in-law Aleksei, who were fighting the Red Army, and their elder daughter, whose whereabouts were unknown. First of all, however, they had to find a place to put down their bags.

The station building was already packed with people, but after a thorough search, they found a good place quite near the station. It was a big glass pavilion that looked as if it had had once been a restaurant. The glass windows had been broken and everything looted except for several wooden benches and tables, but the Borotinskis were lucky to have found a place where they could sit down and relax. They had learned that people who stayed in the station were told to leave in the middle of the night by sweepers.

Valentina, her mother, father, and Olga, with her as-yet-unweaned child, put down the rug and blankets they brought with them, making a temporary home. During the day, their trunk and suitcases served as a table and chairs, and the family felt relatively comfortable.

Their chief worries lay in how to get in touch with the remaining members of the family, how long they dared stay in Russia, and when they should initiate the emigration procedures with the British.

As was her custom, Matushka Maria assumed the role of a leader. Olga, who had her baby to care for, and Valentina, who was pregnant and couldn't move around very much, were content that it should be so.

No snow fell in Novorossiysk, but the winter weather felt bitter cold.

The only food Valentina could find was hardtack and a variety of canned goods supplied by Russia's allies, France and Great Britain. Maria would go to the station restaurant each day to and bring back hot water to make warm tea. The young mother Olga and the expectant Valentina found their warm drink quite delicious and sustaining.

Maria liked to walk about town and talked with people to pick up detailed news about the war situation. One day, she happened to hear that a Red Cross train had arrived from Ekaterinodar. Sania had been working there at a hospital administered by the British, but the family had since lost contact with her. Rumor had it that sick and wounded patients had been left unattended aboard the train, the medics having abandoned them to save their own lives or the lives of their families—a sad instance of man's instinct for selfishness. Maria heard that no one else had stepped forward to help the abandoned patients.

Having heard that the train had come from Ekaterinodar, Maria made up her mind to see for herself. After all, there was a possibility that she might hear some news about Sania. She hoped so.

Early in the morning, Maria took some warm clothes and a bite of food with her and set out to find grain. As she entered the train, a miasmic stench greeted her, and the sight was like a vision of hell, too gruesome to her eyes. Maria forced herself to walk among the sick and wounded who had been left behind, and then, suddenly, Sania appeared before her eyes. Her face had wasted away to skin and bone, but Maria felt no doubt it was Sania.

"Sania!" Maria cried out to her exultantly.

Maria learned afterward from Sania that most of the medics had succumbed to typhus. Those that remained used up all their medical supplies and then went for help, but they never returned. The patients who remained alive gradually weakened and were now on the verge of death. Sania appeared to be half-conscious. Maria fed her the bit of food she had brought and dressed her warmly. Sania could not stand up by herself, so Maria wrapped her arms about her and drew her to her feet. Maria walked her off the train so that she could breathe fresh air. The first day, Maria could do no more than that. For several days until Sania was able to walk, Maria went back and forth to the train. At last, the day arrived when Sania could be brought back to the family at the pavilion.

The day Maria went to fetch Sania home, Valentina went as well to carry Sania's few miserable possessions. The winds of Novorossiysk were cold and blew in swelling gusts that took their breath away. Maria and Valentina walked on either side with an arm around her waist to prevent her from collapsing. When they arrived at the pavilion, people gathered to greet her and expressed their joy at her safe reunion with her family. Sania drank down a cup of hot tea with evident relish. Little by little, Sania began to speak of the nightmarish conditions on the train, the delirious ravings and sobs of people on the brink of death begging for help. When she realized that she was no longer strong enough to get off the train, she, like many others, wished only that death would be swift.

Maria's next triumph was the reestablishment of contact with her sons and son-in-law. Father Valerian couldn't believe that in the normal course of events, such coincidences and strokes of good fortune were possible, yet Maria nevertheless succeeded in finding them.

The munitions supply car aboard which the three men were serving had suffered damage in an ambush and was transported to Novorossiysk for repairs. Having come upon this piece of news early in the course of her daily investigations, Maria immediately turned to searching for the repair site, which she had been told was on a siding. But it was difficult to establish where this siding was situated. Applying her redoubtable persistence and her keen sixth sense, she went from one railway official to the next until finally she met with the army officer in charge of personnel postings and railway movements. From him she learned their whereabouts. Eventually, Nicholas, Modest, and Aleksei made their way to the glass house, and the family celebrated a joyous reunion, all the happier because when last they parted the outlook for their survival seemed bleak.

The White Army had mounted an offensive, and all three were optimistic about their chances for victory. It was decided that they would delay filing an application at the British immigration office. In hindsight, it was much to have hoped for, but at the time, the family was unanimous in its trust that the war could be turned around.

The three men arranged for Valentina and Olga, as well as the other family members, to live in a corner of the armored train that they were attached to. The train was separated into two parts. Before setting off to do battle, the cars containing weapons were uncoupled and went to the front, while the other cars remained where they were. When the ordnance supply train was mobilized, Maria, Father Valerian, and Sania had to go back to the glass house and look for a place to put their things down.

Valentina, along with Olga and her nursling, however, had each been given permission to accompany their husbands and, for the time being, were with their men. They also arranged for overnight quarters in the nearby village on days when their husbands were off duty.

Soon enough, the men began to realize that a White Army victory was no more than a fatuous dream. Nevertheless, both women desired to be with their husbands, and this weighed heavier than any other consideration. Valentina and Olga decided that they would find a place to stay to which their men could come whenever they had time to be with them. They eventually found a house with two extra rooms in a Cossack village.

On the day they moved in, the owner of the house introducing them to his family but warned them to watch out for the Greens, a band of freebooters who belonged neither to the Red faction nor to the White one.

The Greens were men who had become tired of politics and left the Red or White Army to loot and rape as a group. The landlord also warned about feral dogs and the occasional hungry wolf and told the two women not to go out at night, not even to the back garden. That night, Valentina and Olga watched as the wolves leapt over the fence into the garden. Their landlord and some rifle-toting neighbors chased away the wolves. The sight of the Cossacks chasing the pack of wolves by the light of the moon terrified Valentina and Olga. They decided that they had been hasty to settle on this place. The next night, even more wolves came. The two women made up their minds to leave as soon as they could return to stay with Maria and Sania. When Aleksei, Nicholas, and Modest came to spend the night, a band of Greens, who were no more than ravening human wolves themselves, raided the village, looking for plunder. The siren at the village office screamed out its warning of imminent danger. At first, the Cossacks seemed unaware of what was happening, but when they saw Olga and Valentina trembling with fear, the Cossacks went out, each with a rifle in hand. The fight went on right inside the village, and Aleksei and the others went out to chase off the Greens with the Cossacks. Valentina and Olga waited inside, ready to run if they had to. Valentina prayed that she could see her husband and brothers all at least one more time. It was nearly dawn when the men returned, exhausted, and immediately dropped off to sleep. A number of officers and men had apparently been shot to death in the Green attack. The Greens were just one more problem that Russia had to face during this period of internal turmoil. All three men had to return to the front the next morning, and they said that they were likely to be gone for quite a while. A new regulation had been issued requiring the White Army soldiers not to leave the supply train at night.

Olga, Dmitry, and Valentina returned to the glass pavilion to stay in safely with Maria and Sania.

CHAPTER 20

Leaving Mother Russia

Valentina was now in her fifth month of pregnancy and utterly absorbed with the changes occurring in her body. She told herself that she must depend upon her own resources, for there was no one else to whom she could turn. Clearly, if she did not love and protect her baby, no one would. There was also a distinct possibility that the Red Army would prevent Aleksei from ever seeing his child.

General Denikin, commander-in-chief of the White Army, in consultation with the French and British, decided to regroup his forces in Crimea and from there mount a massive offensive against the Red Army. However, White Army losses were already too great to sustain this sort of all-out attack, and the Borotinski women decided to apply for emigration documents at the British evacuation office as soon as possible.

Matushka Maria demonstrated her customary fortitude once more. Olga's baby was not yet weaned, Sania was still recuperating from typhus, and Valentina was heavy with child. Nevertheless, Valentina was the most active of the three young women, and it became her duty to go with her mother to register for exit visas at the evacuation office, which was housed in a converted warehouse. A long line had formed in front of the door, and they resigned themselves to wait for several hours before an official could interview them. Patiently waiting their turn, Maria and Valentina at last made their way through the door and into the converted warehouse. Behind a long table on the far side of the room were seated representatives of both the White Russian and the British armies in military dress.

Maria and Valentina hoped it could be arranged for all of them to go to France, for at least they could speak the language, and also, Madame Simon, Valentina's former tutor in French, had since returned to her home in Paris. However, it was no longer the case, if it ever had been, that refugees could go to the country of their choice. The Red terror was spreading throughout Russia, and people arrived in droves, anxious to emigrate to any country that would have them, no matter where it might be. Valentina and her mother were told to wait a month.

Meanwhile, the White Army was reeling, having suffered defeat after defeat. The women received a letter from their men, advising them not to wait but to leave Russia as soon as they could. The men would know from British emigration records which country they had gone to and would be able to join them eventually.

"A priest is obliged to go where he is needed," Father Valerian insisted, and he made up his mind to stay behind at the British hospital and to maintain contact with his sons and son-in-law.

Maria and Valentina went each day to the emigration office to look for openings to leave the country. At last one day, they were given the wonderful news that a family of the same size as theirs registered to leave in two days but had now decided to stay in Russia.

"Only two days!" Olga exclaimed. She feared that if she left Russia, she might never see Modest again; she felt resolutely opposed to the prospect of such a sudden departure.

"All this talk about being arrested or sent to a labor camp is just nonsense!" she exclaimed. "What's the big hurry? We're in no danger here!"

Valentina hugged Baby Dmitry to herself and stared at the obstinate Olga, who she saw was on the verge of tears. She wondered if it were possible Olga had forgotten the gruesome sight of human bodies undulating in the sea off the coast of Crimea.

"I don't want to leave Russia any more than you do," Valentina replied. "But what kind of life can we expect in a place where people think nothing of crushing you underfoot like a bug! Stay if you like, Olga. But Mama, Sania, and I are going whether you do or not," Valentina chided.

"Well, then, I guess we'll go too," said Olga, and, wiping her tears, she set about in silence packing her things.

Two days later, the four Borotinski women and the infant Dmitry boarded their boat. By now, it was nearly the end of January 1920. The day dawned cold, but there was a gentle breeze and the sun shone brightly, giving promise of a warm day to follow. The ship, with its burden of refugees, glided slowly out of the port of Novorossiysk. Olga and Dmitry were given a special cabin set aside for young mothers. Sania, wearing a scarf to cover her head which had been shaved when she was feverish with typhus, was settled in the ship's hospital. Valentina stayed with her mother.

On deck, people stood watching as their motherland receded astern. With heavy hearts, they thought fondly of family members and loved ones, whom they feared they might never see again. In barely perceptible increments, the coast of Russia sank low on the horizon and then disappeared altogether. The refugees had not been told the port of destination as they sailed off into the Black Sea, only that their ship would first call at Constantinople (now Istanbul), where they would undergo a quarantine inspection. From there, it was anyone's guess, although informed opinion held that likely destinations would be Serbia or Greece.

One consequence of World War I and the fall of the Austro-Hungarian Empire was that a new country had come into being in the Balkans. The Kingdom of the Serbs, Croats, and Slovenes had now been renamed Yugoslavia.

The Serbian King Peter, now sovereign of a greatly expanded realm, and his crown prince Alexander had both been educated in Russia, and they felt a deep sympathy for the plight of the Russian refugees, whom they looked upon as their Slavic brothers. Peter and Alexander provided as much assistance as they could despite the fact that Serbia had suffered bitterly and had fallen into straitened circumstances after the war.

Wherever they were going, as the sun descended toward the horizon, Valentina dozed off with fatigue. Suddenly, there came to Valentina's sleepy ears the familiar strains of the Lord's Prayer, arranged by Rimsky-Korsakov, and a song, *a cappella*, somewhere on the ship. A priest, vested in stole and liturgical cuffs, had begun vespers, and people on deck had risen to their feet and begun to sing the service along with him.

Valentina was now completely awake. Even the British sailors took off their hats, while the captain drew himself up and made the sign of the Cross. Valentina looked around and saw that almost everybody on deck was responding to the service.

As a child of a priest, Valentina had often been witness to the profound effect upon the spirit of the Orthodox services, but never had she participated in such a compelling and spontaneous communion between believers and God. Perhaps most of the refugees borne away from Russia on this ship felt that they might never again set foot on the soil of their homeland.

CHAPTER 21

The First Foreign Land of Refuge

The Black Sea, situated on the fringe of the Mediterranean world, has been known since ancient times for its turbulent waters kicked up by gale-force winter northeasters. For these Russian refugees, however, the seas remained calm, and the only tempests they experienced were of their own making. The voyage thrust Valentina, whether she liked it or not, into contact with people of all stations and outlooks. Some were good-hearted people, noble in their regard for the well-being of their fellow refugees, while others were completely selfish and boorish, concerned only with their own personal welfare.

The British ship carrying the Borotinski women underwent quarantine for a month at Constantinople before heading for the port of Thessalonica in Greece. Many among the Turkish people whom Valentina met during the month spent at anchorage in Constantinople were sympathetic toward the Russian refugees, and some even generously shared what food they had. On the other hand, few of the Greeks that the Borotinskis came in contact with in Thessalonica—despite their being Orthodox—showed much compassion for the refugees at that time. Indeed, many of them saw in the compromised and desperate situation of the refugees an opportunity to extort valuables in exchange for food. Ironically, in the later years, living as fellow immigrants in Canada and the United States, Valentina was to enjoy the friendship of a number of warmhearted Greeks, freeing her at last from a prejudice created during her time of great hardship on the journey out of Russia.

One day, in Thessalonica as the Borotinskis waited with fellow refugees for notification of their final destination, several Serbian Army officers came on board and announced that they would all be going by train to the Kingdom of Yugoslavia.

One consequence of the Versailles Peace Treaty, signed by the combatants following World War I, had been the creation of a new multiethnic nation by adding to the Kingdom of Serbia the former Austro-Hungarian Balkan territories of Croatia, Slovenia, and Bosnia-Herzegovina, the former Turkish territory of Macedonia, and the small independent principality of Montenegro. However, since the sovereign of the new country was a Serb, the Croats and Slovenes felt disenfranchised. Smoldering ethnic resentments would eventually lead to its dissolution in the post-Soviet era.

Valentina knew that even in the best of times, starting a new life in a foreign land would not be easy. Valentina and her family were now starting their new life in the very worst of times, and in addition to that, Valentina was now about to have her baby. Her salvation lay in her eighteen-year-old youthful resilience and in her optimistic outlook on life. She was confident that soon the fighting in Russia would wind down and they would all go back home to carry on with their lives as if nothing had happened. But now prospects were bleak that the day they all prayed for would arrive anytime soon.

Her husband and the White Army were still locked in mortal combat with the Reds. Valentina was desperately aware that she alone would be responsible for the life she was about to bring into this world.

In Surdulitsa, a small town in Southern Serbia, on May 11, 1920, Valentina's first child was born. She named him Boris. Aleksei had chosen the name in the event that the child would be a boy.

In the wake of World War I, much of Yugoslavia's economic infrastructure was in shambles, and its people were living in dire poverty. Thus, it was that the professionals among the refugees—physicians, engineers, and teachers in particular—were welcomed with open arms. It was hoped they would contribute in large measure to the economic recovery of the area.

Two Serbian leaders bestowed numerous kindnesses upon the Russian émigrés, who possessed particular skills. One of these leaders was King Alexander, and the other, Patriarch Varnava of the Serbian Orthodox Church who, like the king, had been educated in Russia. Through their kind intercession, many Russian refugees were appointed to responsible positions. In addition, unemployed refugees were given a modicum of financial aid to tide them over until they found work.

In time, this favor shown to educated and skilled Russians would lead to a backlash of anti-Russian sentiment and the exclusion of White-Russian émigrés from some occupations. Nevertheless, in the early days of the exodus, the Borotinski, along with their fellow emigrants, found safe harbor for their ambitions of a better life.

Father Valerian himself was a prominent beneficiary of Russophile largesse. After seeing off the four Borotinski women, he had stayed behind to serve as a priest in Novorossiysk. But well aware that the crunch would not be long in coming, he too left the mother country and was reunited with his family, eventually finding employment as a priest in a small parish in Skopje, the capital of the province of Macedonia. Of course, the offer of this position did not simply manifest itself out of the blue but was achieved due to Matushka Maria's masterful manipulation of *znakomstva* (connections). As she would say to her children, "a hundred friends are worth more than a hundred rubles."

While still in St. Petersburg, it had been Father Valerian's custom to invite young foreign students of theology to his home and entertain them generously. Hospitality was considered a key feature of the Orthodox home. Among these foreign students were a few from Serbia and Montenegro. After settling in Surdulitsa, Maria dredged up from her long memory the names of Serbian and Montenegrin theology students. She wrote letters informing them that Father Valerian would soon arrive in Serbia to join her. The bishop of Skopje happened to have the same name as that of a student who, long ago, had often visited Father Valerian. Maria wrote to inform him of Father Valerian's plight and received a kind reply from which she learned that the priest who had often visited Father Valerian had long since passed away. However, the bishop, it seems, had at one time studied at St. Petersburg Theological Academy and was grateful for the hospitality he had received in Russia. He promised to do his best to help Father Valerian.

In fact, not only did he find a parish for him in the largest and most prosperous district of Skopje, but he also gave Valerian and his family money to tide them over until they had settled in. This kindhearted bishop with deep pockets later rose to become the patriarch of the Serbian Orthodox Church, but never did he forget Father Valerian.

At the time the Borotinskis had fled Russia, the White Army was retreating into Crimea with the intention of mounting a concentrated counterattack against the Red Army. However, because of the White Army's growing losses and the breather it provided which enabled the Reds to regroup and bottle them up in the Crimean peninsula, the planned counterattack never took place. For several months, the White Army held the Isthmus of Perekop, which connects the Crimean peninsula to Ukraine, but in the cold of winter, the shipping canal that cut through the Isthmus froze over, and the Red Army was able to cross on the ice into Crimea. By the end of 1920, the White Army acknowledged defeat, and the remaining forces were evacuated by allied ships. Some 300,000 White Army soldiers fled Russia at this time. Modest, Nicholas, and Aleksei, who had fought the civil war to its bitter end, were evacuated from Crimea seven months after the women had left and safely rejoined the family in Macedonia. Soldiers who missed the last boats leaving Russia knew they could not expect honorable treatment at the hands of the invading Red Army, and a number of them committed suicide by throwing themselves into the sea.

No sooner had Modest, Nicholas, and Aleksei arrived in Skopje to a jubilant welcome than Matushka Maria set out for Zagreb, carrying a little suitcase filled with documents and diplomas belonging to her two sons, Modest and Nicholas, and her son-in-law, Aleksei. She had heard that there was a better university in the Croatian capital of Zagreb than the one in Skopje or even than the one in Belgrade, the national capital. She decided to try to get all three admitted to the university there.

Zagreb was called Little Vienna because of its many old stone buildings in the Western European style and its tree-lined streets. The main street, lined with stately trees, was particularly renowned. Immediately upon getting off the train at Zagreb Station, Maria could see that the city reflected the high culture of Central Europe and was strikingly different from Macedonia, which was mainly agricultural and strongly influenced by the culture of the Ottoman Turks.

After two days' travel by train, Maria arrived in Zagreb. She went immediately to the university and spoke to several Russian professors, whose aid she enlisted in filling out applications for her three young men. She then immediately set out for home. Not long after, her three sons packed their belongings and headed for Zagreb. Modest and Aleksei were set to study engineering, and Nicholas would study to become a medical doctor.

Father Valerian's salary was not sufficient to pay tuition for all three men, so their women back in Skopje had to work extra-hard to subsidize their men's studies. Sania and Olga worked as nurse' aides, and Valentina and Maria took care of the two little boys and did the housework, which included laundry, cooking, and housecleaning.

The combined three salaries were still not enough to support a big family and send money to their three students. So Valentina decided that she too must get a paying job. In order to get a good job, however, she had to master the official language, Serbo-Croatian, which, though it belonged to the same Slavic language group as Russian, was in many respects quite different. Valentina began studying Serbo-Croatian from a Russian who spoke the language. Macedonian, a dialect of Bulgarian, was used in daily life but did not have the status of an official language.

Valentina often felt exhausted from taking care of the boys in addition to doing the housework, but she was determined to master the language. She studied hard, foregoing a few hours' sleep every night. She had inherited her mother's gift for languages, and soon Valentina mastered Serbo-Croatian.

Valentina's first job as a telephone operator certainly required her ability to speak Serbo-Croatian. One of Father Valerian's friends taught Valentina how to fill out an employment application form and advised her to write "a humble Russian refugee" under her signature. Refugees with high-level skills were treated favorably, but young people without skills could not easily find work.

The job at the telephone exchange required her to work alternate shifts. When Valentina worked afternoons, she could finish her housework before going to work. The night shift, however, was an ordeal. In a small house, where everyone rubbed shoulders with each other during the day, it wasn't easy to rest one's tired body, but once she fell asleep, she slept like a log.

Valentina was young, and she enjoyed receiving money in exchange for her labor. Her pleasure, however, was not to last long.

As everyone had warned, Valentina's husband contracted tuberculosis as a consequence of his lung wound. His condition gradually worsened, and he was soon unable to study. His tuberculosis was diagnosed as terminal, and he came back home to Skopje. As she watched Aleksei kiss and hug little Boris, Valentina began to worry that her son might become infected as well. With a sad heart, she decided that she must separate Boris from his father.

How manly Aleksei had been at the front! How confident and reliable! Even in the midst of civil war, Valentina had been so happy just to be with him. But where had those joyous days gone?

The Aleksei that Valentina saw now was a total stranger who looked out at her from vacant eyes. Valentina's heart turned cold in her breast, and just as everyone had foretold, she began to rue the day she had set eyes on him.

The last straw was her belated discovery that Aleksei was gambling away her hard-earned money. Aleksei agreed to a separation and moved out of the house. He lived with an old Russian man for a while, but every so often, he would come back to see Boris. Valentina pitied him, but for the sake of Boris's health, she turned him away. Her abandonment of her sick husband provoked pangs of remorse that assailed her all her life.

Ignorant of the suffering visited upon her fellow Russians who had chosen not to flee the Reds, Valentina did her best to adjust to life in her new homeland.

In Russia, in 1921 and 1922, the ravages of the revolution and the ensuing civil war brought famine in 1921 and 1922, accompanied by an epidemic of deadly typhus. The economy and the transportation system were in shambles.

Patriarch Tikhon, head of the Russian Orthodox Church, who had remained at his post in Moscow, issued appeals for assistance for the famine victims to all the leaders of the churches. However, his efforts met with harassment from the Bolshevik government. He was eventually detained as a counterrevolutionary and was tortured during his imprisonment. Patriarch Tikhon died at age sixty on April 7, 1925, after he was released from prison. His last words had been "The night will be very long and very dark."

In 1924, Valentina received notice that Aleksei had died alone in the sanatorium in Surdulitsa, where he spent his last days. Boris was just four at the time. Valentina's feelings ran deep at the news of her husband's death, but all she could do was cross herself in silence and pray for the peace of his soul.

Ten years later, Boris mounted a search for his father's grave, but he could not find it.

CHAPTER 22

Macedonia

On December 30, 1922, the Union of Soviet Socialist Republics (USSR) was established under the headship of Vladimir Lenin. Following Lenin's death on January 21, 1924, the secretary of the Communist Party, Josef Stalin, disposed of his rivals one by one as he gradually arrogated dictatorial powers to himself.

When Father Valerian and Matushka Maria learned that upon Lenin's death the name of their beloved city had been changed to Leningrad, it seemed like a final crushing slap in the face of their dear Mother Russia.

Macedonia, where the Borotinskis had settled, was located almost in the center of the Balkan Peninsula and was the southernmost territory in the Kingdom of Serbs (renamed Yugoslavia in 1929). Rich in natural resources and largely agricultural, producing chiefly grapes and tobacco, it was one of the most undeveloped regions of the kingdom. It had been a Turkish possession until the beginning of the twentieth century, when the influence of Islam and the culture of the Ottoman Turks was strong. There were many mosques, and in the evening, the aroma of sizzling mutton fat hung over the town. Having come from the cultured, Western European city of St. Petersburg, Father Valerian and Matushka Maria had difficulty adjusting to their more primitive existence.

The younger members of the family however—though Russia remained in their hearts—resigned themselves to adopting the cultures of the Southern Slavic peoples into whose midst fate had blown them. Valentina now bore the additional burden of being a widow, but Maria helped care for her two grandsons, enabling her daughter and Olga to work.

Boris and Dmitry, though cousins who had both nursed at Valentina's breast, possessed very different characters. Dmitry, who would later study medicine in Vienna and practice as an anesthesiologist in the United States, was the senior of the two by ten months. He was by nature driven by a roguish curiosity, while Boris, who would later become a veterinarian, also in the United States, was gentle and meek. Both had blond hair and bluish gray eyes. The mischief the two got into together was at times quite extraordinary, and narratives in which the two played the questing heroes have been passed down in the family legend. Dmitry was quick-witted with a dash of cunning, but he was never mean. Boris tended toward naivety and was easily lured into adventures conceived by Dmitry. While the two young mothers were off at work, Maria took responsibility for her grandsons, whom she had admitted to a succession of kindergartens, none of which stayed long enough to put down roots. The first was a French school, where, after the boys started going, enrollment plunged, forcing it to close down.

They next attended a Russian school. But one day, Maria received a phone call from the director of the school, a close acquaintance, who begged for a rest from the boys. "In the meantime, *Matushka*," she said, "if you will forgive me for saying so, might you try disciplining your grandsons? Please don't get upset. I have great respect for you, *Matushka*, but watching over those boys is a Herculean task."

There was no point in sending them to kindergarten only to have them thrown out of one school after another. So *Matushka* decided to keep them at home for a while.

One day, the boys brought home a crow with a broken wing, which they were allowed to keep only if they promised to take care of it. For the two boys, "taking care of the crow" meant taking it everywhere they went and feeding it sour cream, cookies, and peppercorns—a regimen likely to kill a crow, and soon it did. Deeply saddened, the boys put their wits together and decided the dearly departed creature required a proper funeral. After wrapping the crow in sheets of newspaper, they dug a hole and buried it. They then erected a wooden cross over the grave and held a service. Donning vestments made of newspaper with armholes cut in them and tying a piece of string around a stone for a censer, they began chanting a prayer just as they had seen their grandfather do in church.

Father Valerian was moved by the boys' praiseworthy sentiment for one of God's creatures. However, as a priest, it disturbed him that a cross had been erected over an animal's remains. At last, Father Valerian struck upon a way to convey the Orthodox belief. He asked them if the crow had ever gone to church before it died. The two boys thought this over but couldn't be sure. At length, they replied that the crow probably hadn't gone to church. "See?" said Father Valerian. "It's not a Christian crow, so you can't erect a cross over its grave." This explanation satisfied the boys, and they dismantled the cross.

There was yet another embarrassing episode the two innocents inflicted on their grandfather, Father Valerian. Father Valerian was in the habit of bringing back sweets for his grandchildren whenever he went out. The boys would always ask him from whom the sweets had come. Father Valerian would always reply, "It is a present from old billy goat, Vasya." It never occurred to Father Valerian that the boys would take him seriously. But being children, after all, his grandsons assumed that a certain kind uncle Vasya, who happened to be a goat, was supplying them with sweets, conveyed into their hands through their grandfather.

At that time in Macedonia, even in a city the size of Skopje, it was not unusual to see a flock of sheep or goats raising a cloud of dust as they were driven out to pasture and blocking the road to traffic. One day, as Father Valerian and Valentina were walking with the two boys, they came upon a group of goats with a red-haired old goat walking at the head of the flock.

"Oh, Grandpa, is that Uncle Vasya?" asked the boys, already convinced it was so. Father Valerian, probably lost in thought, responded with a questioning "Ahh?" which the boys took as confirmation. Immediately, they ran out in front of the goat, which stopped, bringing the rest of the flock and street traffic to a halt. Valentina and Father Valerian watched in astonishment as the boys, with the politeness impressed upon them by their grandmother, bowed deeply to the goat and said, "Dear Uncle Vasya, kind Uncle Vasya, thank you so very much for the candies and cookies you always send to us." Valentina was speechless. Father Valerian disappeared. In his mind, his grandsons were pagans worshipping a goat. Fortunately, the boys had expressed their gratitude to Uncle Vasya in Russian, so the people who had stopped on the thoroughfare merely smiled in amusement at the shenanigans of the two boys and then moved on without any notion of what the boys had said. Valentina shouted angrily at the boys and pulled them up by the scruff of the neck, allowing the goats to amble on to pasture.

On their return home, Valentina told the rest of the family how the boys had stopped a whole herd of goats, how they had bowed politely to "Uncle Vasya," and how Father Valerian had run away in shame. Everyone rolled about with laughter, but Father Valerian never again brought home sweets from Uncle Vasya, the billy goat.

Several months passed since the boys had been asked to leave the last Russian school. However, with Boris and Dmitry always getting under her feet, Maria could do her housework only with great difficulty, so she prevailed on yet another school to take the boys in hand.

By then, winter had arrived. Modest, having finished his engineering studies at the University of Zagreb, had started work as an electrical engineer at an army hospital. He and Olga now lived in quarters supplied by the hospital. Adjoining the hospital, and surrounded by barbed wire, lay the grounds of an army headquarters battalion.

The new school had seemed to be working out well for Dmitry and Boris. Then, one day after work, Valentina went to visit Olga. As the two sat drinking Turkish coffee and talking of this and that, a messenger arrived with a note for Olga from the commander of the military base.

"Dear Mrs. Borotinski," it read, "please don't be worried or frightened. Your son and his cousin have done some mischief and are hiding. We have sent some soldiers to search for them, but the boys are afraid of the consequences and won't show themselves. I'm sure if you should come and call to them they will come out of hiding."

Olga and Valentina rushed to the hospital and shouted to the boys to come out and show themselves. Finally, the boys appeared. Valentina and Olga broke down in tears at the sight of their boys, each wearing only one shoe and with their clothes ripped to shreds by barbed wire.

According to the boys' story, they had been expelled from their new school, so they decided to go to Dmitry's house. On the way, they came upon a horse and cart that carried workers to the hospital, but the driver was nowhere in sight. They got into the driver's seat to see what it was like, but the horse suddenly went off at a trot with the driver, who had now appeared, giving chase. The cart finally came to a halt on the bank of a nearby river. The boys jumped off, crawled under the barbed wire, and ran through the military base to the hospital where, they hid themselves. The story of this escapade became the talk of the town.

At about that time, the house Valentina and her parents lived in was sold and they were given notice to move. After looking at several apartments, Maria found one she liked. The landlady seemed a pleasant woman, but as Maria introduced herself, the landlady's features hardened.

"Are you, by any chance, the grandmother of Dmitry and Boris?"

"Oh yes," answered Maria, proud that this woman knew of her grandsons.

"Oh, I'm so sorry. The fact is this apartment is already spoken for."

Thus was Maria denied tenancy of a new home due to her grandsons' notoriety.

CHAPTER 23

For Love or Money

Valentina felt a deep and brooding discontent at the prospect of year after year working herself to the bone just to put bread on the table, while never being able to buy new clothes or simply sit down with a book. She fell into a profound melancholy that little by little withered her spirit.

If only I had money, she thought, *then all my problems would vanish. If I ever marry again, it will be to someone with money.* Indeed, many were the men who sought the favor of this young and attractive widow. One of them, Mikhail Mikhailovich Puchalsky, a Polish aristocrat, had even asked her to marry him. He was fifteen years older than Valentina, and he had succeeded to extensive ancestral lands in Poland. But something about Mikhail made Valentina feel uneasy.

Maria, on the other hand, was enthusiastic about the prospect of the union. She didn't want her daughter to wake up one day to discover herself approaching old age while still leading the precarious existence of a refugee in a strange land. And so Maria forsook the role of the principled wife of a priest, for that of a mother who had suffered hardship and was worried that her daughter won't have enough money to survive on. "After all," she said to Valentina, "You've already failed once at marrying for love," Maria added. "And, of course, there's Boris to think of too." Eventually, Valentina gave in to the pressure and agreed to marry her admirer.

Valentina was twenty-three years old when she remarried. She moved into Puchalsky's big house in Prishtina, the administrative center of the Kosovo region, where a live-in German maid attended to all her needs. Since leaving Russia, Valentina had endured extreme poverty, and it seemed, at first, that she had entered a dream world where there was money enough to buy anything she fancied. She wore the most exclusive French perfumes and dressed in haute couture clothes ordered from Paris. She now considered herself a lady of the aristocracy to whom the notion of gainful employment was axiomatically abhorrent.

As she settled into her new life, she gradually came to feel that behind the thin veneer of luxury, her life had become meaningless and her inner yearnings unsatisfied. She discovered, as well, that her husband was a philanderer and a violent drinker who struck out at those about him. But what hurt her most was his cruel treatment of her beloved Boris.

Valentina now felt that she had made a huge mistake marrying this man. Her one wish now was to live a quiet life, free from dependence on this or any husband. She felt ashamed for having sold herself into a life of ease. Thereafter, Valentina felt an intense contempt for anyone who married for money, as she had. To her, the idea of such a marriage seemed tantamount to an act of prostitution.

After more than two years Valentina divorced Puchalsky. It would be no exaggeration to say, however, that, except for a brief period in the early months of the marriage, not a day went by when Valentina wasn't made to weep bitter tears.

Her marriage to Mikhail had taught her a lesson she paid for each day with hot tears: High birth and wealth can be just as painful as poverty, and life holds no guaranteed happiness. At length, Valentina concluded that personal independence and a good education could be the sole means by which she could establish herself on a firm footing in life.

Valentina decided to attend a university. She put Boris in an excellent cadet boarding school in Bela Crkva, a small town near the border with Romania. The school administrators charged the children of Russian refugees a mere pittance, yet provided them with a good education. Valentina then enrolled herself at the Skopje University. It was 1928, and she was twenty-six years old when she divorced Puchalsky and returned to her parents' home. She had to pay her own tuition, so life was again difficult for her, but now she gloried in her hard-won poverty and devoted herself to her studies.

At Skopje, Valentina studied German literature and comparative literature. She preferred to study French literature since it was her favorite foreign language, but that course of study required knowledge of Latin, which she lacked, and so she chose German instead.

Valentina was fortunate and met the renowned scholar of Russian literature and authority on comparative literatures, Evgeniy Vasilyevich Anichkov, who had been on the faculty of St. Petersburg University before the October Revolution. Valentina was ecstatic at having the opportunity to study under this famous scholar. Back in Russia, she could never have dreamed even of meeting him. Professor Anichkov recognized Valentina's unusual gift for languages and so hired her to assist him with publishing his lectures and translating some of his works into Serbo-Croatian.

She also gave private lessons to augment her income. Life was not easy, but she was happy.

Valentina would often discuss literature late into the night with her fellow students and professors. Among them, the artist Alexander Burin. Sasha was a gentle, good-natured Russian with whom Valentina established a particularly close relationship. It warmed Valentina's heart to see how well Sasha got along with Boris when he came home from school on vacations. She hesitated, however, to consider getting married for a third time, telling herself that for the time being the most important thing for her to do was to finish her course of study at the university and get her diploma.

During these years, a tumult of events took place in her adoptive homeland. In 1928, Stefan Radich, the leader of the Croatian faction, was assassinated in Belgrade by a Serb deputy while parliament was in session, triggering the formation of a strong Croat separatist movement. The Croat deputies left Belgrade and formed their own parliament in Zagreb, Croatia. King Alexander responded, early in 1929, by assuming absolute power and changing the name of the country from the Kingdom of Serbs, Croats, and Slovenes to the Kingdom of Yugoslavia.

Valentina also heard that in October of that year, 1929, far away in New York, share prices on the Wall Street financial market plummeted and panic spread through the Western world.

Eventually, on June 9, 1932, Valentina graduated from the University of Skopje, but there were no jobs, not even for those with a university diploma. Valentina managed to survive for two years by continuing to tutor language students and by working for Professor Anichkov.

In the end, however, Valentina's dream of becoming a teacher bore fruit, and she found a full-time job teaching French and German at a school in Split, an ancient city on the Adriatic Coast. She left her parents' house in Skopje and headed for Split.

The room Valentina rented in Split had a balcony from which she could look out over the deep blue Adriatic Sea. Boris was still in boarding school, and she could see him only during vacations, but compared with her hectic student days and the ensuing two years of poverty, she now had time to savor her life, and indeed, an encounter she had long awaited was about to change her life.

In the meantime, Olga, the beautiful wife of Valentina's elder brother Modest, had embarked on a career as a singer and stage actress. Occasionally, Olga would give parties, to which she invited admirers and show business people. At one such party, Valentina was introduced to a Russian forestry engineer, Vladimir Mikhailovich Lyovin. Although she had had admirers, Valentina had long been wary of marriage and cherished the freedom of single life. Nevertheless, she fell in love with Vladimir the moment she met him, and he too with her. An Orthodox Christian, Vladimir — his name derives from the Russian for "lion" and Valentina were married on November 24, 1934, at the Serbian Orthodox Church in Split by Father Sergei Urkano. Valentina was then thirty-two years old, and Vladimir some six months younger. It was his first marriage.

Vladimir had been born in Baku, Azerbaijan, to a Russian Imperial Army colonel, scion of a minor aristocratic family, and a school teacher. From a very young age, Vladimir had been sent with his two elder brothers to the Imperial Cadet

School in Sumy, a small town south of Kharkov in Ukraine. At the age of sixteen, he joined the White Army and fought the Reds.

Upon leaving Russia, he worked first as a laborer in Sophia, Bulgaria. Then he was hired by the Bulgarian Orthodox Church to read the Russian classics to an archbishop with failing eyesight who had been educated in Russia and possessed a deep love for its classical literature. Vladimir later enrolled in a Russian cadet school that had been opened for Russian students in Bela Tsrkva (Serbian for 'Whitechurch'), and here he finished his high school studies, which had been interrupted by the Civil War. He then went on to study forestry engineering at the University of Belgrade. After graduation he worked as an engineer for a German-owned lumber company based in Sarajevo, the capital of Bosnia-Herzegovina.

Valentina could not help but love her Vladimir. He was generous to a fault; he took immense pleasure in the company of people, and he had a wonderful sense of humor. When they were together, time seemed to stand still; such joy did she feel when she was with him.

Before the revolution, it was considered unusual for the daughter of a priest to marry a man of the hereditary officer class. The clergy considered military men to be drunkards, gamblers, and womanizers who thought religion concerned only those who died in battle. For their part, the military men saw the clergy as wet blankets who were forever hectoring them to forego the good things in life while they thrived on services they read for the dead. Ironically, even among exiles, the Russian revolution produced a classless society, in which the old prejudices fell by the wayside, thus making the marriage between Vladimir and Valentina possible.

CHAPTER 24

Dalmatia

In Split, Valentina rented a room and soon developed the habit of reclining on a couch on the veranda while looking out over the sea. Here she would lose herself in reminiscences of her native St. Petersburg, which had now been renamed Leningrad. Her memory of her native city seemed to have become merely a borrowed collection of fading photographs. How she wished, just one more time, to behold across the Neva River that sweeping view of the Winter Palace and its flanking buildings.

Valentina had at last come out of the long dark tunnel of grinding poverty into a bright new world of prosperity and hope. Not only was she now financially independent, but by the grace of God, she also had a loving husband with whom to share her joy in life.

The one shadow falling across Valentina's new life was cast by the unfortunate circumstance. Her beloved third husband, Vladimir, worked in the forested areas about Sarajevo, the capital of Bosnia-Herzegovina, while Valentina had to work in Split. In order to spend a few days together, either Vladimir had to visit Split or Valentina had to go to Sarajevo.

The girl's school at which Valentina taught had been founded by Austrians. It enjoyed a reputation for high standards and excellent teaching. "The Modern School for Girls" was derived from the fact that the students' modern European languages were taught, as opposed to classical schools where Greek and Latin were emphasized. The teacher of French and German had taken a two-year leave, and Valentina, who was qualified in both languages, was hired to teach in her absence.

With a full-time job paying a respectable salary, Valentina could rent a room in a hillside house owned by one of her colleagues. Valentina felt wonderfully fortunate to be able to look out over the sea from her window. A port city on the Adriatic and the site of a fourth-century palace built by the Roman emperor Diocletian, Split is steeped in history. Off the beautiful, sun-drenched sea coast are numerous small islands. The school placed few constraints on its teachers. After completing their pedagogical duties for the day, they were free to swim, walk among the Roman ruins, or to enjoy their lives as they wished.

In the Soviet Union, however, there was little joy. One by one, Stalin disposed of potential rivals among Party officials. Beginning with the deportation of Trotsky and the assassination of Kirov, Stalin instituted harrowing witch hunts of supposedly disloyal citizens. Valentina heard that it was said that during the Great Purge, as many as 20 million people were executed or allowed to die in concentration camps.

The Soviet government also ratcheted up its suppression of religious belief, and one after another, the churches and synagogues were taken over by the government. By 1932, in Moscow alone, out of 560 Russian Orthodox churches,

90 percent were being used as museums, clubs, schools, or storehouses.

At the Split Modern School for Girls, Valentina was treated warmly, not only by the principal but by her colleagues as well. Among them, a middle-aged teacher of Croatian origin named Anka Berus became a particularly close friend.

Serbian was spoken in Serbia and its capital city Belgrade, as well as in the provinces of Montenegro and Bosnia-Herzegovina, while Croatian was spoken in Croatia and its capital Zagreb, as well as in Dalmatia. These two languages are, in fact, quite similar and linguists referred to them as Serbo-Croatian. Although Valentina spoke fluent Serbian she soon noted that there were differences between the Serbian she spoke and the Croatian dialect spoken in Split.

There existed a deep-rooted cultural antagonism between the Croats, who, historically aligned with Western Europe, espoused the Roman Catholic faith, and the Serbs, who were Orthodox Christians strongly influenced by Byzantium, and who had endured some five centuries under the rule of the Ottoman Turks. Valentina noticed that the use of certain standard Serbian expression evoked an abrupt and intense estrangement from her Croat acquaintances. The Croats clearly felt superior to the Serbs and did not disguise their contempt for the oriental influences on the language and culture of the Serbs.

Hoping to master those characteristics of Croatian that distinguished it from Serbian so that she could avoid offending her students and colleagues, Valentina asked her friend Anka Berus, a teacher of Croatian, to give her lessons.

Anka was married to a Slovenian, but Valentina had the impression that they were not on good terms, and Valentina noticed that Anka's husband, who taught elsewhere, was hardly ever at home. Valentina also noticed that Anka didn't seem to get along well with her fellow teachers. Valentina had no idea why this was so, and even her landlady, who was an incorrigible gossip, wasn't disposed to satisfy Valentina's curiosity.

Anka was close to the principal, and Valentina thought perhaps a romance might have developed between them. Perhaps for that reason people were reluctant to talk about her. On the other hand, their fellow teachers may have been reticent to speak out because Valentina was Anka's close friend. With Anka's help, Valentina mastered the subtle differences between the two branches of Serbo-Croatian and was soon speaking Croatian like a native.

The principal thought highly of Valentina's approach to language teaching. Although Valentina used the direct method, she supplemented it with the didactic intervention of Croatian to give her students a solid grounding in grammar. Her methods found favor with her students as well. In time, her colleagues began to invite Valentina to their homes. A number of them were witty and cheerful people who liked to dance or sing lilting Dalmatian songs. Valentina took great pleasure in their gracious Mediterranean-style social life, which was quite new to her. Anka, too, sometimes appeared at these parties, but people seemed to feel uncomfortable around her.

In the 1930s, Yugoslav women had not yet won the right to vote. Valentina was indifferent regarding the issue, but Anka insisted it was important for social reform that women be enfranchised. Occasionally, Valentina allowed Anka to take her to a suffragist meeting.

At these gatherings, Anka left Valentina to her own devices and spent the evening in conversation with the meeting organizers. As Valentina was not personally engaged in the issue of women's suffrage, the meetings bored her. On one occasion, she asked Ruzha, another of her friends and the wife of a policeman, to keep her company at a meeting.

Valentina's thoughts tended to dwell on her marital bliss, and it was of domestic matters that she talked about with Ruzha, ignoring the speeches. All she recalled of the meeting afterward was that some men stood around looking ominous and that all the festoons and flowers decorating the hall were red. She also noted a policeman in uniform at the entrance who, when the meeting got underway, suddenly vanished. Next, she heard someone shout, "It's a police raid!"

Ruzha, who had insisted on sitting by an exit, stood up and ran out of the hall with Valentina in tow. When the two women arrived at Ruzha's house, Ruzha's husband laughed and said, "I was just about to go and retrieve you two ladies from jail."

Anka explained to Valentina that although the government opposed women's suffrage, she felt that suffrage was necessary in order to improve the lives of the poor and uneducated of Yugoslavia, where, particularly in underdeveloped areas, illiteracy was most common among women. Hearing that the movement was in aid of the poor, Valentina felt a warm respect for Anka's idealism.

As for Anka, she came to realize that it was impossible to engage the ingenuous Valentina on political issues and so sought to help her in another way. Anka suggested that instead of paying her for Croatian lessons, Valentina should teach her Russian. Valentina thought this odd, for few people in Croatia were interested in learning Russian, and it seemed all the stranger when it became apparent that Anka already knew a great deal of Russian.

The lessons at Anka's house were often interrupted by unexpected visitors who were never introduced to Valentina but were sent away after a conversation in Italian too fast for Valentina to follow. Soon, Anka had Valentina translating Russian texts into Croatian. In her innocence, Valentina persisted in believing that Anka was no more than a peaceable idealist who, out of the goodness of her heart, was working to improve the lot of women by winning for them the right to vote.

Summer vacation came, and Valentina went to stay with her husband Vladimir in Sarajevo. He loved his friends and had many everywhere he went. Among his close friends were a public prosecutor and his family, who had invited Vladimir and Valentina to their home for dinner shortly before Valentina resumed her teaching duties. For some reason, the prosecutor seemed intensely interested in Valentina's life in Split. He asked her question after question about the school where she taught, her colleagues and students, and even the names of bookshops she frequented. The former tenant of her rented room had left a bookshelf full of French books, none of which she had previously read, obviating any need to buy books.

"The fact is," the officer said, "the police in Split chanced to acquire a list of names of Communist Party members. According to the report, a bookshop in Split is disseminating communist propaganda. I wondered if you knew anything about it. It seems some of your colleagues and students are involved with the Communists."

During the train ride back to Split, Valentina ruminated on this and, upon being met at the station by Anka, immediately reported the stunning news she had heard from the conversation she had with the prosecutor to Anka.

Anka turned deathly pale. As soon as she finished carrying Valentina's luggage to her room, Anka rushed away. Valentina had once been told by a senior colleague that Anka was suspected of being a member of the outlawed Communist Party. Valentina knew this couldn't be so. Just to make sure, she had asked Anka, who denied it outright.

"I support a movement that seeks solutions to social problems, but I am not a Communist Party member, nor am I involved in any political activity except women's suffrage."

Valentina had seen no reason to doubt her and had all but forgotten the matter.

The next morning when Valentina arrived at the school, the principal was waiting for her in the hallway.

"Would you mind taking Anka's classes for her?"

"What's wrong with Anka?"

The principal remained silent.

"She came to meet me at the train station yesterday and seemed perfectly all right."

The principal lowered his voice and said, "You had best keep it to yourself that she came to meet you at the station. It might prove inconvenient for you. Anka was arrested at three o'clock this morning. It turns out that she's the secretary of the Dalmatian branch of the Communist Party."

The principal went on to say that Anka had destroyed every piece of incriminating evidence before the police had picked her up. Valentina felt faint. If Anka confessed under interrogation that she had got rid of the evidence because of information Valentina had passed on to her at the station, she herself might also be arrested.

"What a fool I was to trust Anka!"

All of Valentina's colleagues now gave her the cold shoulder. She missed her husband terribly and couldn't sleep at night.

Ruzha's husband, a police officer, was confident of Valentina's innocence and kept her informed about Anka's case. It seemed Anka steadfastly refused to cooperate with the police and, in spite of continuing interrogations, neither revealed any information about her activities nor named any associates. The police were particularly eager to learn who had informed Anka that her arrest was imminent, thus giving her time to destroy her records of Party membership and other evidence that was necessary to bring a case against her and her comrades.

Valentina was desperate to keep the police from learning about her unwitting role in the incident. She had at one time considered her life in Split as the closest thing to paradise. Now overnight, it had become hell on earth. Her happy, carefree days were no more. Her peace of mind had unraveled. Furthermore, because she was known to be close to Anka, her mail was read by the police and envelopes reached her hands already opened. The social club she had been thinking of joining rejected her application for membership.

Valentina could endure the strain no longer and went to Ruzha's husband for advice.

"I can't bear living under this pall of suspicion. I want to tell the truth and prove to everyone that I'm innocent."

Ruzha's husband, however, thought this strategy unwise. "Once you are taken into custody and they start cross-examining you, you are liable to admit to things you didn't say or do. The wisest course is to go on just as always and pretend that nothing has happened."

The school year was drawing to a close. Valentina was so busy with her teaching duties that the Anka affair finally receded to the back of her mind.

One day, the parents of one of her less-capable students sought an interview with Valentina. The student's father said that as an employee of the police department, he was aware of Valentina's involvement in illegal political activities. He threatened to take action against her if his daughter failed Valentina's class. His words brought Valentina to a fever pitch of anger, and her body shook with rage.

"I have never participated actively in any political movement. Yes, I did attend several meetings, but that was because I did not fully understand what they were about."

Her pent-up frustration poured out in a torrent, and she could not stop herself.

"I have done nothing wrong, so I'm not afraid of you. If you mean that I am a friend of Anka Berus, it is true. After all, she is a colleague of mine. However, from what I hear, she never said to anyone that I was a member of the Communist Party. And for my part, I never dreamed that she was a member, either. But this has nothing to do with your daughter's grade. It is dishonorable of you to attempt to use your influence to intimidate me like this."

She was astounded at her own boldness in speaking out. It was as if a cry of righteous anger had sprung up itself from deep within her. The father of the student left quietly.

The months went by, and the end of Valentina's two-year stay in Split drew to a close. Through what process Valentina never learned, but she was cleared of suspicion of being a Communist, and those among her colleagues who had avoided her began once again to talk with her.

In June 1936, Valentina put Split behind her and moved to Leskovats, Serbia, where she found a new position. Because of the Anka affair, Valentina did not expect any fancy farewells and so had bought a second-class train ticket. However, one of her colleagues advised her to exchange it for a first-class ticket since there would be many people at the station to see her off. All her students and most of her colleagues turned out to wish her "bon voyage," bearing gifts of flowers and chocolates. Valentina was touched and could not stop crying.

Eleven years later, in the summer of 1947, Valentina and her younger son, Anatole, and niece, Natasha, were vacationing in the Dalmatian town of Dubrovnik, a beautiful resort on the Adriatic Coast. In the Middle Ages, it was a prosperous city-state that rivaled Venice in wealth and power. Its ships were laden with precious cargoes, called argosy, a corruption of "Ragusa," the Latin name of the city.

During her stay in Split, Valentina had become acquainted with a woman who had rooms for rent in Dubrovnik, and in later years, it became her custom to spend the summer there with her family.

One day, as she made her way to the beach past a mansion that had been turned into quarters for vacationing Croat Communist Party members, Valentina was peremptorily ordered by a security guard to return the way she had come. Valentina persisted, explaining that she was just going to the beach, but the man replied, "The Finance Minister, Madame

Anka Berus, is going to the airport, and we must keep the road open for her car."

She turned and walked a few steps back and then paused, wondering if she should ask to meet Anka so that she could say something cynical like, "Thanks for all you did for me back in Split."

She then thought the wiser of it and, as she walked away, turned over in her mind other much happier memories of her two years in Split.

Anka Berus indeed served from 1945 to 1953 as the first woman minister under Tito.

CHAPTER 25

Under Nazi Occupation

On November 13, 1938, a baby boy was born to Valentina and Vladimir. They had named the baby Anatole. Valentina was teaching in Leskovats, a Serbian town near the Bulgarian border, where Vladimir had been assigned.

In the summer of 1939, when Anatole was not yet one year-old, Valentina's elder son Boris came home on vacation from Belgrade University, where he was studying veterinary medicine. Vladimir was doing fieldwork in Donji Milanovats, where he would remain until the autumn rains made forestry work difficult. Since Vladimir could not come to them, Valentina decided to take her two sons and visit him in the field.

However, In order to get there, located in the wooded region of northern Serbia, one had to travel up the Danube by boat. Most of their fellow passengers were German tourists. Valentina watched as they wrapped their leftover bread in white paper — which they appeared to have brought for this very purpose — and take it back from the dining hall to their cabins. Yugoslavia had a largely agricultural economy and, particularly in Serbia, food was plentiful and inexpensive. Seeing these well-to-do Germans hoarding their bread made her feel lucky she lived in Yugoslavia.

Great mounds of every variety of fruit or vegetable were on sale in the market. Customers could buy a sheep, have it slaughtered and skinned, sell the skin for the price of the sheep, and so have the meat for free. Serbian sausages were sold by the meter, and wine and plum liqueurs, or *rakia*, were quite inexpensive. At the outdoor restaurants, the sweet strains of Gypsy violins could be heard late into the night. Valentina learned from returning travelers, however, that in Germany not only luxury items but even staples were being rationed and that the political climate was extremely tense.

Vladimir took Valentina and Boris for a walk in a park on the banks of the Danube. As they sat together on a bench, Vladimir listened to Valentina recount what she had seen on the boat, and they talked over the situation in Europe.

"When you see tankers carrying more and more oil to Germany, it's obvious what the Germans are readying themselves for. War is inevitable," said Vladimir gravely.

The situation in Europe was indeed grim. Germany had annexed Austria in March 1939 and then had occupied Czechoslovakia. Now Hitler was getting ready to invade Poland.

Perhaps in part, due to Vladimir's dark forebodings, Valentina and Boris did not like Donji Milanovats. Even the beautiful blue waters of the Danube did not soothe Anatole, who suffered from colic, and Valentina cut short their vacation to go back to Belgrade to take him to a doctor.

During this trip, Matushka Maria, who was then living in Ripan in Serbia, unexpectedly died. The cause of death was infected bedsores, which she had incurred as a bed-ridden victim of arthritis and Parkinson's disease. She was only sixty-three years old. She might have lived much longer if she had had better medical care. She was buried just outside of Iverskaja chapel in Belgrade.

When the telegram arrived notifying Valentina that Maria was dying arrived in Leskovats, Valentina was in Donji Milanovats, and so it did not reach her in time for her to go to Maria's bedside. It saddened her that she had not been at her mother's deathbed nor attended her funeral. Only her sister-in-law Olga, who took care of Maria, and Father Valerian had been with Maria at the end. Maria had been a tower of strength for her family. She had been ever present to save her children from their follies and misadventures.

Poor mother, thought Valentina. *She protected me from beginning to end with a love that was fierce and unbending, while I continually defied her.* Valentina had long felt that her mother didn't love her as much as she loved Sania, who excelled in everything she did. But in recent years, this childish grudge had fallen away, and she realized that her mother had taught her many things that had helped her through life. She now regarded her mother with only warmth and admiration.

In 1939, soon after Valentina had returned from her vacation, the German army, without formally declaring war, attacked Poland. Great Britain and France, in response, declared war on Germany initiating the maelstrom of World War II that drew nation after nation into its maw. At least for the time being, however, Yugoslavia managed not to become involved.

The following year, 1940, Valentina learned that her brother Nicholas was dying of cancer. He called Valentina to his deathbed and asked her to care for his family when he was gone.

Nicholas and his wife Nina, the daughter of a wealthy Russian merchant had two girls, Natasha and Masha. For ten years, Nicholas had served the poverty-stricken town of Klisura as its doctor near the border with Bulgaria. Life was not easy. The region was undeveloped and his patients very poor. Serb doctors could avoid working in impoverished rural areas, but Nicholas, being a Russian refugee, had no choice but to live and work where Serb doctors chose not to go. An additional disadvantage for Nicholas was that towns and villages along the nearby Bulgarian border were subject to occasional attacks by Bulgarian terrorists.

One day, when Valentina was visiting Nicholas, she heard Nina complaining about their lack of money to Nicholas. He had just come back from a house call.

"I'm sorry, dear," he said. "They seemed so desperately poor. I didn't have the heart to take their money."

These words revealed to Valentina Nicholas's generous and compassionate nature as well as his crushing poverty. He had been a heavy drinker since his youth, and now Nicholas was dying of liver cancer. He died at the age of forty-two. Valentina was surprised by his parting words just before his death.

"I do not have long to live," he had said. "It is the time for me to report to God." Nicholas saluted in jest. Valentina had always thought Nicholas was an atheist, but these last words disclosed that he was after all a believer. Valentina cried with happiness. She promised Nicholas that she would take care of his family.

Upon his death in August 1940, he was accorded a funeral with full military honors by the Serbian military command in Nish.

In the spring of 1941, the Yugoslav regent, Prince Paul, signed a treaty with Nazi Germany and Fascist Italy. The pact allowed German and Italian troops to cross Yugoslavia in order to attack Greece, which was then successfully defending its border with Albania against attack by Italian troops. Most Serbs considered the treaty with the Nazis to be a shameful betrayal of their ally Greece. Demonstrators took to the streets shouting, "Better war than ignominy!"

The demonstrations and rioting ushered in the army's rebellion and the fall of the government. The ignominious pact was immediately rescinded. Hitler responded in April 1941 by attacking, in league with the Italians, without having declared war. Belgrade and other major cities were subjected to punishing air raids. The Yugoslav Army took the field but was swiftly overrun, and Yugoslavia ceased to exist.

The German occupation inflicted major changes on the curriculum at Valentina's school. Now the German language became compulsory subject in the curriculum. Many of the students refused to attend classes. The principal, although he prohibited the teaching of French, did not punish students who boycotted German classes.

In Donji Milanovats, Vladimir could hear the sounds of shooting once in a while. Guerrillas hid in the forest outside the town and occasionally attacked Germans, who, it was rumored, had threatened to kill a hundred Serb civilians for every dead German soldier. Vladimir was a forestry worker. He would have been among the first to be sacrificed. He resigned his job and moved with his family to Belgrade where he found work for the Julius Meinl Company, an Austrian-owned purveyor of foodstuffs.

Life in Belgrade was not easy for Valentina. Her sister-in-law Nina and her two daughters now lived with

Valentina so that made three more mouths to feed. Poor little Anatole continued to suffer from chronic stomach pains.

Because the Nazis had closed all the universities, Valentina sent Boris to Germany to work. The Germans had promised to give scholarships to foreign nationals who worked until the war ended.

There was a serious shortage of food and fuel. One day, Valentina discovered that in her absence Vladimir had torn pages from her beloved *English-Serbian Academic Dictionary* in order to make a fire. It was more than she could bear. Breaking into tears, she cried, "You barbarian!"

They cooked their daily meals on a brazier set up on a little concrete veranda, which doubled as a storeroom. They had to be careful that nothing unintended caught fire. The family kept an odd assortment of things on the veranda, and when life became a bit easier for them, they even kept geese there.

One evening, as Valentina prepared a supper of powdered soup and eggs for the children, she noticed a young Serbian woman looking over at her from a similar veranda on the other side of the street. After a while, a German officer came out on the same veranda and asked in German what she was doing.

"I am cooking supper for my children," Valentina answered in fluent German. The officer was impressed by her excellent pronunciation, and they carried on a conversation that led to an offer of a job working for the German Army.

Although she would have preferred other employment, her hunger prompted her to reply swiftly in the affirmative. The German officer told her where to appear for an interview the next day. The following day, Valentina had eaten no breakfast and had only a slice of bread with tea for lunch. By the time she finally arrived at the building housing the regional Civilian Rations Office for her interview, she felt weak and dizzy. Fortunately, there was an elevator to carry her up to the fifth floor. The officer who had invited her to come was very kind. He gave her a sheet of paper with a column of numbers on it and asked her to add them up using a manual calculator. Valentina made short work of the task, and, satisfied with her secretarial skills, the officer left the room.

Next, a German woman came in and explained the work Valentina would be doing. She praised Valentina's German and by way of instruction did a portion of her task for her. Valentina then followed the woman's instructions to the letter and finished up the job. After that she was too weak with hunger to proceed to the next task. Malnutrition had given Valentina a low resistance to infection and had caused her to develop a painful boil on her buttocks. She explained her situation to the German woman and asked to be excused for the rest of the day so that she could put an ice bag on the boil.

The German woman then asked about her family and Valentina replied that she had three hungry children, a sister-in-law, and a husband to feed. The woman went out of the room for a moment and came back with a sheet of paper and held it out to Valentina. It was a ration voucher on which were written all the things that Valentina would now be qualified to receive at a ration center. She would be able to get sugar, flour, oil, and even vegetables. Valentina could hardly believe her eyes. The woman then took her to the cafeteria and gave her a solid meal, the likes of which she had not eaten in many a month.

When Valentina arrived home, she showed the paper to Nina, who for a moment was speechless. That very day, Nina went to the ration center and returned with so much food she could hardly carry it all. Dinner that day was a feast of sausages, freshly baked bread, and other delicious foods.

Valentina's new job involved arranging the monthly distribution of foods produced at two processing factories supervised by the German Army to every workplace in occupied Serbia. Rations were allotted according to the number of people at each workplace and in the aggregate amounted to millions of units of measure. Responsibility for distribution to individual workers, however, lay with local officials, and Valentina's office remained unaware of malfeasance unless a grievance was filed.

There are always people who are intent on lining their own pockets in wartime. Yugoslavia was no exception. Grievances, in fact, fairly flooded into Valentina's office. They came from workers complaining that they had not received the quantity of food to which they were entitled. Everywhere, black markets offered attractive profits to unscrupulous people.

When Valentina's office received a complaint, it went first to the German officer who was the chief administrator. He thought about how the case should be disposed of. Normally, if a thorough investigation revealed that the local Serbian bosses had sold the workers' rations on the black market, the case would be handled by the Gestapo, the dreaded Nazi secret police. If the amount of food stolen was significantly large, the punishment was correspondingly severe. Sometimes thieves were executed. Cases of large-scale theft, however, were normally considered outside the purview of minor non-German workers, such as Valentina.

Once, however, a major grievance came to Valentina's section when the officer in charge was away from Belgrade. Some forestry workers claimed they had not received food rations for two months. Because their grievance had not been accepted at the local office, they came directly to the German headquarters in Belgrade to petition for redress. Valentina took notes regarding the main points of the case. She suddenly gasped in surprise. The name of the Serb official against whom the grievance was directed was quite familiar to her. *Why! This is the very man I went to see before the war about getting a transfer for Vladimir!*

It had been very difficult for Valentina as a teacher and Vladimir as a forestry engineer to find jobs in the same town. Vladimir's Serbian colleagues were reluctant to work in a small town and could finagle an assignment through their cronies to a more populous area.

Consequently, Vladimir, a Russian outsider with no contacts, always ended up getting transferred to rural areas, where customarily there was no high school. This meant she could only be with her husband if she gave up teaching. Moreover, Valentina was afraid that her husband, who was quite attractive to women, was having affairs when she was not with him.

In order to get a job in a big city, it was important to know what other people were doing to get a job. Applicants needed to know the secret routes to the administrators in the offices of the Ministry of Forests and Mines and also in the Ministry of Education, who would accept bribes.

One particular incident had happened some years before when Vladimir had once again been transferred to a small town where there were no high schools. Valentina decided to take things into her own hands and appeal directly to the offices of the Ministry of Forests and Mines in Belgrade.

When she arrived at the ministry, the guard at the gate asked her to relate her purpose in coming.

"It's no use going to see an official directly about such a matter," he advised. "It's better if you go to his house with a nice present for his wife."

Valentina did not think that the sort of gift she could afford to buy would have any effect. She remonstrated with the guard, arguing that the law protects the right of husband and wife to live together. But he only shook his head and said, "It's no use, I'm afraid."

Valentina ignored the guard and waited for hours before she was at last allowed in. In a tremulous voice, she pleaded, "My husband and I always end up being separated. I don't care where it is, but could you please arrange things so we can both work in the same town."

The official coolly replied, "There's no one available to go to the town where your husband is working. To put it simply, nobody wants to go there, and your husband has no connections to make someone go in his place. You might as well give up."

"You mean he was sent there merely because he has no connections?"

"Exactly! But that's life. You see, somebody has to work there."

"What about our family life? A married couple has the right under the law to live together. Do you mean we'll have to live apart all our working lives?"

"That's right. As they say, absence makes the heart grow fonder. And meeting once or twice a year makes the honeymoon last longer," he added with an insolent snicker.

Valentina would simply have been merely disappointed had he not responded with this lewd insinuation. Without saying another word, she turned on her heels and left. "Bora Nikolich, I will forget neither your name nor your insult," she vowed silently.

When Valentina read the name Bora Nikolich on the petition regarding food distribution, she recalled the humiliation he had once visited upon her. It was clear to her that Bora Nikolich and his cronies in the Forestry Department were selling the workers' rations on the black market. These crooks thought the workers wouldn't have the courage to take their case directly to the Germans.

After the delegation of workers left, Valentina rang up the Forestry Department. The phone rang. She waited. Eventually, she heard the voice of the man whose name she had sworn not to forget.

"We've just received a complaint from your workers that they've not received their food rations for more than two months. How can that be? Where are the rations we delivered to you?"

She listened to his excuses, uttered in a trembling voice, and then cut in to further tighten the screw.

"By the way, aren't you the Bora Nikolich I asked to arrange a transfer for my husband, Vladimir Lyovin?"

There followed a deep silence on the other end. Valentina could almost feel Nikolich's panic as he considered what might happen to him if she took her revenge and reported his crime to the Germans. Valentina, however, was not a vindictive person nor was it in her purview to pass judgment on the case. She had put a scare into him, and that was enough to satisfy her. She told Bora Nikolich that she would hold on to the petition for a few days to enable him to buy back the food and distribute it to the workers who would then report to her office that the misunderstanding had been cleared up.

Bora Nikolich had no recourse but to do as she advised. Thus, through Valentina's generosity, Bora Nikolich was spared a visit from the Gestapo.

One day, Valentina took Anatole to the Danube to swim. She was utterly shocked to see corpse after corpse float by on the current. She immediately pretended to Anatole that she had a stomachache and hustled him home before he could comprehend the gruesome spectacle.

She later learned that the dead bodies were victims of a massacre by the Croatian fascist group, Ustashi, who had attacked a wedding party at a Serbian Orthodox Church on the Croatian side of the Danube.

In April 1941, with the occupation of Yugoslavia, Croatia became a German puppet state. The Croats, who had long resented Serbian dominance in Yugoslavia, were rumored to be planning the assassination of one-third of the Serbs in their territory. They also planned the conversion to Roman Catholicism and of one final third would be exiled to Serbia. The Serbs retaliated by cruelly persecuting the Croat minority in their own territories. Thus began the practice of "ethnic cleansing" that again and again has bloodied the map of Yugoslavia.

About 170,000 people died in Yugoslavia during World War II, and fully half of them were victims of genocidal murder committed among ethnic groups.

In February 1943, Valentina's father was shot in the back at his home one night as he lit a kerosene lamp. He was seventy years old.

There are two likely explanations for his murder. First, Father Valerian openly held the Germans in contempt. He owned a radio, which was a rare item at that time, and he used it to listen to BBC anti-Nazi broadcasts. It is possible that someone had reason to report him to the Germans as a suspected Communist spy.

Another possible reason was that after Matushka Maria died, Father Valerian lived alone, with only his housekeeper coming regularly to the house. She happened to be a Croat and a Catholic, whom Father Valerian protected from those Serbs, who wanted to avenge on her their fellow Serbs residing in Croatia. Hence, the murderer may have been Serbian monarchist Chetniks who at that time were collaborating with Germans in carrying out attacks against the Croat minority in Serbia.

A housekeeper woman found Father Valerian's body the next morning and called the police. By that time, his corpse was cold, however, and there was no trace of any murderer. The gold cross Father Valerian never parted with in life was missing, but it appeared that robbery was not the primary motive for his murder.

Of his four children, the second son Nicholas had predeceased him. The eldest son Modest and his wife Olga were living in Vienna with their son Dmitry. Valentina and her elder sister Sania were the only close relatives still living in Yugoslavia. Valentina asked the police to investigate her father's death, but no one was arrested.

Father Valerian had died a violent death in a foreign land. He was buried by another priest in the town of Ripan in the churchyard, where he had served as pastor to the Orthodox faithful in the declining years of his life.

The letter informing Valentina of Father Valerian's death reached her two weeks too late. The priest said that he had spent a certain sum of money for the funeral and asked for reimbursement, if at all possible. Valentina and Nina paid the full amount.

Valentina's share of inheritance from Father Valerian consisted of a 100-pound pig and three hens. She renounced her share in favor of her nieces, Natasha and Masha. Their mother Nina went to Ripan to retrieve her daughters' inheritance. Nina had the animals butchered and was advised not to return to the Belgrade railway station but to get off around Topchider and find her way home from there instead. In Belgrade, the authorities were checking incoming luggage looking for such goods such as pork and chicken that would have been confiscated. All day, Valentina and her nieces worried about Nina's return trip. Finally, Nina burst into the apartment. She had been almost hysterical with fear as she hurried all the way from Ripan while carrying the food. Valentina cooked the meat, and they all enjoyed its fresh flavor.

Modest and Olga were contenders for Father Valerian's golden cross and Matushka Maria's silver icon; none of the items were found. Valentina initially exchanged letters with them, but she soon felt so disgusted with their greed that she stopped writing to them.

One day, Valentina was summoned by the Gestapo. "What did I do wrong?" she asked Vladimir and Nina, who suggested all possible reasons. Valentina soon found herself within the scary walls of the Gestapo, where she discovered that none of those possibilities were the case.

The problem was a complaint from Vienna from her brother Modest Borotinski. He had asked the Gestapo to help him get his inheritance. Valentina burst out laughing and told the officer where the alleged inheritance was supposed to have been. The officer began to laugh too. Valentina asked him to write back and advise Modest to go to Ripan himself to search for the cross and the icon. Valentina heard nothing more from Modest and Olga until the end of the war. Nobody ever mentioned the inheritance again.

CHAPTER 26

Belgrade

As the autumn of 1944 deepened into winter, Adolf Hitler's ambitions for a global empire began to collapse on all fronts. The population of Belgrade, which day after day had watched allied bombers droning high overhead toward the Ploesti oil fields in Romania, now looked on in silence as the Germans fell back in orderly retreat toward the fatherland. By mid-October, the Soviet Army had advanced south across the Danube into Yugoslavia and was pressing on toward Belgrade. Since being driven out of Sevastopol in April, the German Army had experienced defeat repeatedly at the hands of the Russians, and now Tito's Communist partisans had joined the fray on the side of the Soviets.

On Easter Sunday, following the onset of crippling air raids on Belgrade, Valentina sought refuge for her family in the suburbs of the city. But as the front drew ever nearer and farm cottages became strong points of the German defenses, it became apparent that Valentina and family would be safer elsewhere from the mortar and small arms fire now being rained down on them by the advancing guerrillas. Valentina and family moved back into their former apartment at 30, Tsara Dushana Street, which was within walking distance of the old Turkish Kalemegdan fortress in the northern quarter of Belgrade near where the Sava River joins the Danube.

One day, as the rattle of machine guns grew louder in the distance and columns of black smoke rose here and there in the city, a group of German soldiers approached Valentina's building with the apparent intention of setting up a machine gun. It was obvious to all that as soon as the emplacement fired on the advancing Russians, Valentina's building would be targeted for an artillery barrage, and it would surely be reduced to rubble. Valentina summoned up her courage and approached the soldiers to establish elsewhere.

"Please don't put your guns here," she pleaded in German. "It will scare the children. There are babies here too."

The corporal commanding the machine-gun squad gave her a sharp look and retorted, "Are you Communists?"

"No! No! We're White Russians who ended up here after escaping from Russia during the civil war. They'll treat us like traitors and shoot us on the spot. Give us a chance to save our children."

As the Germans discussed what to do, Valentina caught the eye of one of their member who stood apart from the others. He approached Valentina. "I'm a Frenchman from Alsace," he said. "The Germans claim it as historically theirs, and so I was drafted and have to fight for them," he said in low tones. Then, in response to a few words of French from Valentina, he went on in his native language. "I wish I could take this uniform off," he said, "but they're always watching me. I'm just another German to the Russians, and they'll shoot me."

Since the poor Frenchman's situation was much like her own, she begged him to suggest to his comrades that they find another spot for their machine gun.

"*Oui, madame,*" he replied and rejoined his fellow soldiers.

Perhaps due to the Frenchman's intervention, the squad of machine gunners left and never came back.

When the German's battle for the city escalated into house-to-house fighting, Valentina and the other tenants moved down into their building's damp basement for a week. From the windows, all they could see were the feet of soldiers running past the building and the school across the street. The Germans had confined some of the Greek priests in the basement.

Valentina's family had anticipated that there would be a pitched battle for control of the streets. She had bought quantities of food, which they shared with those of less foresight or means. Soon her family's supplies began to run low, and Valentina grew increasingly anxious about what was going on outside. It was impossible to tell, even in the daylight, on which side a soldier was fighting, just by looking at his feet as he ran by the window firing his weapon.

One day, Valentina heard the Greek priests shouting from their basement window that they didn't have any food or water. The Germans had left them to starve. Although Valentina begged him not to go, Vladimir put some food in a bag and dashed across the street drawing fire from all sides. Fortunately, he came back alive.

Valentina and Vladimir were doubly apprehensive about the imminent arrival of the Red Army. Not only did the Soviets consider all Russians who had fled the motherland during the revolution to be enemies of the people, but also Vladimir, at the tender age of sixteen, had joined the White Army. On top of that, he had been a member of a corps of Russian volunteers organized to help the Germans quash the Communists. Vladimir had initially believed that Hitler wished only to liberate Russia from the Communist yoke. Soon, however, events led him to realize that the goal of the Germans was, in fact, to conquer new lands and to enslave Russia. Fortunately, by feigning feeble-mindedness, he had been able to secure his discharge before being sent to fight Tito's Communist guerrillas. If they should ever come to know of it, the Soviets would still consider his temporary enlistment a serious crime.

Valentina too had worked as a clerk for the Germans, and that alone would prompt the soviet to charge to her with having been a collaborator. She would be punished or imprisoned.

As Valentina's family cowered in their cellar, they began to hear voices shouting in Russian. Red Army soldiers were trying to communicate with the Serb citizenry. Among these voices, Valentina clearly heard someone calling out Vladimir's name. She couldn't help wondering how they got it and what they wanted from him. Fearing the worst, Valentina's legs weakened beneath her.

However, she need not have worried. One of her Serb neighbors had told the Soviets that a Russian family lived nearby, and they were calling on Vladimir to help them. Vladimir presented himself to some officers, who showed him a map and asked him how to get to the Kalemegdan fortress, where German resistance was still quite strong. The fortress, just a ten-minute walk from where they were, was situated on a hilltop and controlled troop movement over the prospect below. It had served many armies in the past as a strategic position and was now being used by the Germans to cover their retreat.

They asked Vladimir to lead the way to the fortress. Although it was a dark moonless night, Germans were now sniping from housetops, and they had set up ambushes on the route to the fortress. As the point man guiding the Red Army troops, Vladimir was risking his life to help them. Valentina scarcely drew a breath until her dear brave Vladimir was safely home again.

Valentina was also concerned about the effect of these terrible events on young Anatole. Although he was a quiet and sensitive child, Anatole wasn't frightened by the Soviet soldiers. For some of them, perhaps, he served as a surrogate for children of their own back home. Besides, he spoke fluent Russian. So eager were the Russian soldiers to share his company, they vied with each other to ply him with chocolates.

There were two Red Army soldiers who made a particularly strong impression on Valentina. One of them was Pavel, a lieutenant billeted in her building. His troops were responsible for patrolling the approaches to the fortress at night for the duration of the battle. Pavel explained to them that the Germans were putting up a stubborn resistance, and the area around the Kalemegdan stronghold, including Valentina's building, could still not be considered secure and might at any moment come under German attack. Hearing this, Valentina felt a shiver run down her spine. It meant that if the Germans learned there was a Soviet unit billeted in the building, they might at any moment zero in with the artillery and reduce the building into rubble.

Pavel offered to detail some of his troops to evacuate Valentina and her family. Pointing at Anatole, he said, "It's for his sake." Valentina thanked Pavel for his kindness and, after hurriedly packing, put three suitcases outside the door of her apartment building. Valentina's watchful Serb neighbors lost no time in shouting to Pavel to take them along too.

A German sniper on the roof of a nearby house heard the commotion and started shooting. Some of Tito's partisans were sent to dispatch the sniper, but he succeeded in holding them off. A single artillery round would have taken care of him, but it would also have caused civilian casualties.

In the meantime, Valentina had put her family's bags on the truck. Pavel then told Valentina to wait inside the apartment, while he went around the neighborhood to assure the Serbs that he would return with more trucks to carry them to safety as well. When Pavel came back, he wore a huge smile. "The Germans have just surrendered Kalemegdan," he told Valentina. She would no longer need to evacuate.

Sometime later, a huge Soviet tank rattled to a stop in front of Valentina's apartment house. All the residents crept out onto their verandas to take a look at this monster. Some of the tank crew clambered down, and Valentina invited the soldiers in for a drink. After a while, one of them staggered back to his tank. A neighbor of Valentina, who had given the tank crew drinks, started screaming hysterically. "He's going to shoot!' she shouted. "He's going to shoot!"

As everyone scrambled to get back inside the building, they heard a deafening report. The whole building shook. Mortar rained down on everything from the stucco ceiling in the foyer. Most of the apartment windows were shattered. Valentina willed herself to open her tightly closed eyes and saw Anatole standing in the foyer, safe and sound, but covered with plaster dust.

Shouting angrily, Pavel ran out of the house, pulled the drunken crew member from the tank, and slapped his face.

"You drunken idiot!" he yelled. "What are you doing? You've frightened the civilians! And on top of that, you've injured one of your comrades!"

A good-natured Armenian soldier named Sasha had been standing under the cannon's muzzle when it was fired. The flash singed his hair and burned his face. Luckily for him, he had closed his eyes, and they had escaped harm. His ears, however, were not so lucky. Later, he told Valentina that he couldn't hear a thing for days.

Valentina stood in awe of Pavel's noble bearing. *Thank God*, she thought, *that even in the Red Army, there are honorable men.*

Sometime later, Pavel took Vladimir aside and spoke to him in confidence. "We don't want to know who you are, why you are here, or what lies in your past," he said. "We are mere soldiers. Our job is only to fight. But beware of those who come after us. Just in case you're thinking of going back home to Russia," he added, "forget it."

At the time, both Valentina and Vladimir were uncertain as to what Pavel meant.

Soon after Pavel's unit left Belgrade, a mournful-looking Soviet soldier began appearing at their door. When he first appeared, he hesitated to step inside. He looked about him, then down at his feet, seemingly at a loss for a single word of salutation. Valentina thought he had come for food but found out that was not the reason. Like many soldiers before him this soldier was drawn to Anatole and would spend hours with him. Valentina noticed a sad smile playing on his lips as he watched the boy marshal his toys about the apartment floor. Whenever soldier showed up, Valentina would make something for him to eat, but he ate nothing and never took his eyes off Anatole. The man looked so very sad that Anatole was a little bit frightened by him. With a sigh, the soldier would eventually rise to his feet and hand over a bag to Valentina saying, "Please give this to the boy." Then he would leave. In the bag Valentina found food. Where had he gotten it, she wondered. Did it come from a bombed out German warehouse?

One day, appearing out of the blue, as was his habit, the sad soldier took a seat and began talking about himself. He was the father of two sons. One day, German soldiers came to punish his village for aiding anti-Nazi guerrillas. The Germans tied his hands behind his back and forced him to watch as they threw his sons down the well. The guerrillas retook the village, but it was too late to save his children. Somehow he survived and joined the Red Army as it moved westward.

"Those who come after us," of whom Pavel had warned, at length arrived. Soon the dreaded NKVD, the Soviet secret police, summoned Vladimir for an interview.

The Soviet Army had replaced the Germans, but this brought little joy to the civilians of Serbia who were hungry and war-weary. There were still food shortages, rationing, and long lines to buy bread, milk, and vegetables. For a time, there wasn't a piece of meat to be had. Weakened by hunger, the local residents now submitted to a reign of terror. The secret Soviet police, summoned, interrogated hundreds of residents and sent them to prison or labor camps. Some were summarily shot.

Vladimir was called in and interrogated at length about his membership in the Russian volunteer corps of the German

Army. The NKVD major who questioned Vladimir seemed to know everything he had done and told him that he was lucky he'd got out of the corps before it engaged Tito's partisans in combat.

"Otherwise," warned the major, "instead of sitting here having a polite conversation, you'd be on your way to a labor camp in Siberia."

The major went on. "You're lucky," he said. "You have an alternative. If you cooperate and tell us what your Yugoslav colleagues are up to, we'll leave you in peace. You can stay in Yugoslavia and work as a forestry engineer as you did before the war. Don't force us to send you to Siberia. The Yugoslav government has given us a free hand to deal with all Russian émigrés in Yugoslavia. Nobody can save you or protect you. Think it over carefully."

Vladimir was astonished by what the NKVD man was telling him.

"Aren't the Yugoslavs your allies now?" Vladimir asked. "Why on earth would you need someone to spy on them for you? What can a forestry engineer possibly find out that would be of any value to you?"

"Today they're our allies" was the major's cryptic reply.

"But tomorrow, who knows?"

Vladimir's first thought was that he could never agree to spy on his Yugoslav colleagues. After all, Yugoslavia had provided him with a second home after he emigrated from Russia. Seeing that Vladimir was firmly resolved to turn down his proposal, the major eased up on him.

"Please, please! No rash decisions now that you might regret later," he said. "You have a family to worry about. We'll give you a week to think things over. Come back the same time a week from today and let us know your decision."

A week later, on the dreaded day, Vladimir got up early. He hadn't told Valentina about the predicament that faced him, but because he was determined to turn down the NKVD proposal, he had to prepare Valentina for any eventuality.

"This is the last time I'll go to see them," he told her. "I have no idea what they plan to do with me, but if they attempt to coerce me, I will resist," he said. "The consequence of that may be that I won't come home. Take care of our son."

Vladimir then packed a small suitcase containing a change of clothes, a toothbrush, and a bar of soap and went to meet his destiny.

What did he mean by "resist"? Valentina wondered, but his stern expression had warned her off asking. Her sister-in-law Nina advised her to go to church, which she did, and when she came home, Vladimir was there waiting for her, a beaming smile on his face.

"When I got to the NKVD offices, there was a big sign on the door saying that the Soviet Army had occupied part of Germany and that the NKVD had followed in their footsteps."

Vladimir was never called in again. Some years later, a number of Russian émigrés were arrested by Tito's secret police, tried, and executed for spying for the Soviet Union. The NKVD had apparently recruited a sufficient number of moles.

CHAPTER 27

Slovenia and Montenegro

In the aftermath of the war, food shortages led to malnutrition and the deterioration of public health, allowing disease to cut down a wide swath of the population. Among them was Valentina's niece Masha, her brother Nicholas's daughter, whom Valentina had taken under her wing along with her elder sister Natasha, and their mother Nina. Masha contracted tubercular meningitis and was carried off in a matter of months. Twenty-five years earlier, Valentina had driven her first husband Aleksei from their house for fear that the tuberculosis that was slowly killing him would infect their child Boris. In 1946, Anatole tested positive for the tuberculosis infection, and desperate to get Anatole out of the damp lowlands, which popular wisdom held to be a breeding ground for the tubercle bacillus, Valentina made up her mind to take him to the Slovenian Alps, which were situated along the border with Austria and Italy.

 She sent off a letter to the Slovenian Ministry of Education requesting that for the sake of her son's health, she be posted to a school in the highlands. To her surprise, she received a swift reply from the ministry, informing her that she would also be hired as a teacher of Russian. German and French were not taught in the immediate postwar period. The position they offered was in the beautiful town of Kamnik at the foot of the Alps some 16 miles north of the capital, Ljubljana.

Slovene belonged to the southern Slav family of languages, which includes Serbian and Croatian. The area had been ruled for centuries by the Austrian Hapsburgs, and the majority of the Slovenians were Roman Catholics. Life with Anatole in the little town of Kamnik, surrounded by pristine alpine peaks, lasted only a year. It was a happy time for mother and son, both of whom quickly picked up the Slovene language.

The principal of Valentina's new school, a Slovenian woman who was a member of the Communist Party, treated Valentina as a friend and intellectual equal. Every morning and evening, the view of Kamnik's snow-covered Alps helped Valentina to dispel memories of the harsh wartime years, and she entered a period of spiritual renewal. She enjoyed living in the quiet country town and found her work with the disciplined and polite Slovenian students to be rewarding.

Anatole turned eight years old in Kamnik. His health improved rapidly. After school and on weekends, mother and son would walk the fields and mountain trails, inhaling the fresh air of the "Slavic Switzerland." Valentina also found it charming on winter mornings to watch the students skiing down from the hills to school. Her niece Natasha, who was studying business in Belgrade, would often come to spend her vacations, and on Sundays, very early in the morning, Valentina would take Anatole and Natasha mushroom hunting or berry picking, as she had done back home on summer vacations spent in Finland.

Her only regret was that she was separated from Vladimir. Otherwise, she would have been content to remain in Kamnik forever. She even had Anatole write a letter to Comrade Tito, begging the "Great Leader" to bring the family together by transferring the boy's father to Slovenia.

The official who reviewed Anatole's letter must have had a taste for irony because soon afterward Valentina received notice that in September 1947, she would be transferred to Nikshich in Montenegro.

In those days, both Slovenia and Montenegro were part of Yugoslavia, but they differed in almost every other respect. Montenegro, or *Tsrna Gora* in Serbian, meant "Black Mountain." It was a rocky, infertile land. Montenegrins were essentially Serbs with an anomalous history that included independent nationhood. They were very proud of their wars of resistance against the Turks and of their national costume, which included the "yatagan," a decorative dagger. The fez, also a part of the national costume, had a Turkish crescent on top with an encircling black band to remind every Montenegrin of the fifteenth century defeat of the independent Serb kingdoms by the Turks at Kosovo.

Montenegro was still largely undeveloped in comparison with Slovenia with its strong ties to Western Europe and its industrialization, so few people from other regions came to work there.

For Valentina, who was used to the cultured, refined, and peaceable Slovenians, Montenegrins seemed roughhewn and arrogant. The quality of her students there was also seemed inferior. Some of them, instead of studying, resorted to bribery or even blackmail to influence their teachers' estimation of their work. Moreover, Montenegrin society appeared to Valentina to be male-dominated and overly macho. The Montenegrin man's dream of the good life involved long afternoons spent smoking his pipe and exchanging bigoted opinions with other idlers over cups of Turkish coffee while his much younger wife drudged in the fields.

Vladimir and Valentina had hoped they would be able to begin and end their days sitting down at the same table to share a meal and spend their nights in the same bed, wrapped in each other's arms. But that dream was not to be. Vladimir's position required him to spend weeks at a time, traveling, while his wife was left to deal with an unfriendly social environment at home. As a teacher, Valentina had always expected her students to work hard and to display the same intellectual and personal integrity that she herself possessed; in Montenegro, they did not. Despite the pressure, she refused student bribes. She ignored threats of reprisal from their parents. Some of the parents were prominent Communist officials, but Valentina would not be swayed. When she awarded the students a poor grade for poor work, she received numerous anonymous letters criticizing her unbending attitude. On one occasion, a student who had failed one of her classes threw stones at her house. Valentina's landlord, however, happened to be a prominent citizen in the town, and he filed a complaint. Thereafter, the police made regular patrols in her neighborhood, and Communist Youth League members escorted her to and from school. Nonetheless, the harassment persisted. Anatole received a few pummelings from disgruntled students avenging themselves over poor grades from Valentina.

On June 28, 1948, the Yugoslav Communist Party, led by Marshal Tito, was expelled from Cominform (Communist

Information Bureau) for Titoism (the defiance of Soviet Supremacy). The whole world watched with bated breath, but Tito held firm against Stalin's pressure while obtaining sufficient support from the West to forestall a Soviet invasion.

During this period of tense relations between Russia and Yugoslavia, many of the Russian émigrés who had maintained Soviet citizenship were expelled to one of the Soviet satellite states on Yugoslavia's perimeter. Valentina's family possessed Yugoslav citizenship papers, so at least on this occasion, they were not treated as outsiders with secret agendas.

Once, however, Valentina was called by the Montenegrin secret police to appear for interrogation. This was done as a matter of routine in cases of suspected anticommunist activity. And because Valentina was a teacher and was in a position to influence young minds, the authority felt an added urgency to review her case. The night before her scheduled meeting, unable to sleep, she cast about for a way of presenting her situation in the best light. As she thought, she was suddenly reminded of a student of hers in a night class who was rumored to have joined the secret police. The next morning, she asked to be interrogated by this former student of hers. After a lengthy wait, she was led into an office, where he was waiting for her.

"Why did you tell them you wanted me?" he led off.

"Because I trust you more than I do anyone else here."

"Good. Then please answer my questions straightforwardly. But don't be surprised if I adjust your responses," her former student said with a broad grin.

Valentina nodded in agreement.

After a few formal questions, the interrogation was over. As Valentina was leaving the room, her interrogator smiled and said, "I used to be so scared of you whenever we had a test."

"I was so scared about coming to see you today," Valentina confessed, and they both laughed.

There was one thing, however, which she had not mentioned to the secret police. She never informed them of the location of her eldest son Boris.

In actuality, Valentina herself had instructed Boris to find work in Germany, and this he had done at first. He wrote her several letters from Germany, but she had not heard from him since the war ended. She did not know his whereabouts. Valentina had even asked the Red Cross to search for Boris, but she had learned only that right after the war, Soviet troops had found his documents in a garbage dump at one of the more notorious Nazi concentration camps. The Soviet investigators assumed that he had perished in the camp, but Valentina had never abandoned hope that he was still alive.

1948 Christmas drew near. In the Communist nations of Eastern Europe, every obstacle was placed in the way of its celebration. In Yugoslavia, anyone who missed school or work on Christmas Day was punished with a stern warning. Valentina, who had a reputation of doing exactly as she pleased, was specifically told to spend the day watching over the boarding students. Vladimir had been assigned to special duties that disallowed all possible pretexts for a day off, and for Anatole as well, it was school as usual.

For some reason, the students at Valentina's school appeared to be feeling a particularly infectious variety of Christmas spirit that year. Their high spirits distracted them from their studies. Nobody dared to come right out and say, "Merry Christmas!" but it was clear that the students were thinking of gifts and Christmas joy that awaited them at home. The principal and other teachers who belonged to the party made a show of being exasperated with the students for not keeping their minds on their studies. Still, most of the teachers hesitated to punish the students' passive resistance to the ideological ban on Christmas.

Valentina hesitated to teach on Christmas Day, so she retreated from her classroom to the teachers' lounge. A young Russian woman among her colleagues whispered in her ear, "The mailman brought a letter with a foreign stamp on it. I grabbed it thinking it was for me, but it's addressed to you. You'd better sit down as you open it."

This was at a time when you could be blacklisted if it was found out she had relatives in a foreign country. Valentina couldn't trust even her best friend.

The letter was postmarked at Giessen, West Germany. The sender's name was her dear boy Boris Zhukov! With trembling hands, Valentina opened the letter. Yes, it was unmistakably Boris's handwriting. But to protect her, the persona he had adopted was that of a mere acquaintance rather than her son. Valentina had almost given up hope of ever seeing him again, and this letter made her so terribly happy. Boris was alive! Someday she would see him again! "Thank God, he's still alive!"

Valentina felt deeply grateful. Here in a country where no one could celebrate Christmas openly, what greater gift than this, whose meaning only she could decipher!

CHAPTER 28

Leaving Yugoslavia

Valentina decided to leave Yugoslavia. After Valentina received the Christmas letter from Boris telling her that he was alive and well, another letter arrived from her niece, Natasha. This letter was to irrevocably change her life. Natasha's letter informed Valentina that in the spring of 1950, Natasha and her mother Nina had been granted exit visas to leave Belgrade for the Free Territory of Trieste. Trieste was under the administration of the United States and Britain from 1947 to 1954, pending resolution of a dispute between Italy and Yugoslavia over its sovereignty. Natasha's letter opened Valentina's eyes to the fact that emigration from the Federal People's Republic of Yugoslavia to free world might be possible for her as well.

Natasha wrote that after graduating from a business college in Belgrade, she had gone to work for a government trading company. On occasion, she would tell her coworkers ironical anecdotes that she had heard from her uncle Vladimir about Tito's Communist dystopia. Evidently, someone had reported her to the authorities. One day, as she was walking home from work, she was picked up for questioning by the secret police.

She spent several hours in the cellar of an old, soot-stained building, waiting for her name to be called. Eventually, at the close of her interrogation, she was warned that if she continued to ridicule the government, she would be cruelly punished. In the meantime, she was told to appear once a week to report on the activities of her superiors to an agent assigned to her case.

Natasha's mother, Nina, who had heard earlier of this opportunity for Russian émigrés to leave Yugoslavia for the West through the Free Territory of Trieste, applied for exit visas, which were immediately issued. Wasting no time and without telling a soul, mother and daughter hurriedly packed a few belongings and left for Trieste.

Valentina's chief reason for wanting to leave Yugoslavia was to give Anatole the opportunity to obtain a good education and be able to choose his future occupation freely. Under the educational system established in Yugoslavia, one of the duties of a teacher was to serve as a member of an endorsement committee, which determined the occupation most suited to each student's ability. But over and above a student's academic potential, a teacher was required to consider social background, character, and political maturity, the latter a cant term for loyalty to the Communist Party of Yugoslavia.

Academic ability was important, but it was not the sole standard determining if a student would be permitted to attend a university. Top priority for these few treasured places was assigned to the children of Tito's partisans who had fought with him against the Germans. Next in line were the children of Communist Party members. Finally, came the children of peasants or factory workers—children of the bourgeoisie, former officials of the Kingdom of Yugoslavia, priests, or other enemies, the proletariat. The only way that those who fell into this terminal group could get a professional education was to agree to take a post that students with better qualifications shunned, such as a country schoolteacher or dentist.

Even if Anatole were a brilliant student, the best he could hope for was admission to a teachers' college in some provincial town, where he would be eyed with suspicion as the offspring of an enemy of the people. After graduation, he would be posted to a backwoods school where he would remain until he retired.

In order to give Anatole a chance to shine, Valentina decided to leave Yugoslavia. Ever adventurous and courageous, Vladimir supported Valentina's plan to leave the country. He took charge of applying for exit visas on behalf of the family. They decided it would be best not to admit that they currently held Yugoslav citizenship. They also chose to use their former address in Belgrade on the application instead of their address in Montenegro. This would simplify the bureaucratic ramifications for obtaining visas. The submission of these two pieces of false information, however, if uncovered by the authorities, would result in the family's immediate arrest.

Vladimir took a few days off work and set out for Belgrade. When he arrived at the visa office early the next morning, he found the atmosphere tense. The clerks were testy and hurled insults at the applicants. One by one, they completed their business and slipped out the door, leaving only Vladimir. He was obliged to return within twenty-four hours to Montenegro; he had but one day to apply for their visas. He sat patiently for hours in the waiting room until a gruff-voiced clerk opened the door and barked, "Don't just sit there like a bump on a log! Hand over your application." Vladimir did so and was told to come back the following day for the visas.

The next morning, he was handed his visas, and he hurried back home to Montenegro.

As she studied the exit visas, Valentina mused over what the future held for them. Could anyone be so lucky! Once she had an exit visa, she could cross the border to a refugee camp. Once she got that far, she could ask to immigrate to a third country. This little piece of paper could get her out of Communist Yugoslavia and into Italy. From there, you could go anywhere you liked, even to rich countries like the United States, Australia, or Canada. She realized that dreams *do* come true.

As she contemplated the future, ever-brighter visions of days to come filled her imagination.

When Valentina told the principal of her school that she was leaving, her announcement was met with disbelief. The principal shuffled his papers and began to describe the courses he intended Valentina to teach in the coming school year. Even her family doctor, a Croat of elegant sensibility, smiled cynically and attributed her announcement to an overstimulated imagination verging on the delusional. After all, who had ever heard of a nonparty member leaving Montenegro for the West? Why, it was incredible and utterly ridiculous!

Only two people believed her. One was her landlord, whom Valentina had always thought a shrewd man, and the other was the manager of the food distribution office who was responsible for issuing ration coupons. As soon as the landlord heard that Valentina was leaving, he arranged to rent their rooms to somebody else to prevent the local government from assigning a Communist Party functionary to the apartment. The ration clerk informed her that he would stop issuing coupons to her from the end of the month. Valentina sold their few pieces of furniture and packed the family's suitcases.

A police officer, who was engaged to the landlord's daughter, showed up and reminded them of the formality of notifying the police of their intention to go on a trip. Anyone traveling, even within the province, had to go first to the police and report where they were going, for what purpose, and for how long. The police would then issue a document that had to be shown to police everywhere that a person went. Vladimir went to the police department to file his statement but came home angry and discouraged. The police had confiscated their exit visas until they could verify the documents' validity. Valentina was desperately worried. What if it were found out that they had made false statements? The new tenants were waiting for them to move out of the apartment, and their food rations had been canceled. On top of that, they had both quit their jobs. The mere mention of exit visas would mark them as pariahs wherever they went, and they might very well end up as homeless wanderers.

Kind neighbors took care of Anatole and shared their food with him. The landlord's daughter was sympathetic and let them stay in her room.

Vladimir was paralyzed with indecision. He hesitated to aggravate the police by asking that the visas be restored to him, but the expiration date on their visas was drawing near. If they didn't make it to the border in time, they would have to apply for extensions. After considerable brooding over the alternatives, Vladimir decided to go to the Montenegrin Ministry of Home Affairs in Titograd, the provincial capital, in order to leapfrog over the local police in Nikshich.

All they had left of any value were two wristwatches and a pocket watch which Vladimir gave to Valentina, saying, "If I don't come back, sell these and go appeal to Tito himself in Belgrade to let you go."

Valentina thought this an absurd thing to say but nodded through the smoke of her cigarette. She had taken to smoking during the war in order to steady her nerves.

Around noon the next day, Anatole came running into the room with a piece of paper.

"It's a telegram from Papa!" he shouted.

The telegram read, "Back soon with visas."

They took the first train from Nikshich to Sarajevo in Bosnia-Herzegovina, where they changed for Belgrade. Sarajevo was a place of happy memories for Valentina, who used to visit Vladimir there when they were first married. In Belgrade, they stayed for a few days with friends in their old building at 30, Tsara Dushana, where they had lived during the war. Then they said good-bye to all their friends.

On the train heading for the Italian border, Valentina, now forty-eight years old, reflected at length on the thirty years of her life that she had spent in Yugoslavia. After leaving Russia, there had been a very short period of married life with her first husband Aleksei. Then came Macedonia, where Boris had been born and raised, then Serbia, where her parents, who had hoped to go back to Russia, were buried. Later, there was Prishtina in Kosovo, where she had lived with her second husband Mikhail for a short time, and Skopje, Macedonia, where in her late twenties, she had studied so diligently at the university. Next was Split, Dalmatia, where she had got her first job, teaching languages. In Belgrade, her knowledge of German had won her a job with the German army during the occupation. Slovenia also held fond memories, with its woods and views of the Alps where she had lived so happily with Anatole. Finally, there was Montenegro, which she had detested. Of course, in addition, there had been Dubrovnik, in southern Dalmatia, "the Pearl of the Adriatic," where her whole family, including her niece Natasha, spent several wonderful summer vacations. All these places held memories of so many encounters with enchanting people!

Yugoslavia, my second homeland, Valentina thought, *it is unlikely I will ever see you again*. Tears welled and spilled down her cheeks for everyone in the train compartment to see.

In September 1950, several days before their exit visas were to expire, the family crossed the border and entered the Free Territory of Trieste, sandwiched between Yugoslavia and Italy.

Vladimir told her later what had happened in Titograd. He had been very worried as he waited to be received by the Minister of Forestry and Agriculture of the People's Republic of Montenegro. He had no idea what he would say to get him off the hook and restore the visas back to him. As he was led into the office, the minister looked exceedingly annoyed.

"I really do not understand what those bureaucrats in Belgrade are thinking! Here in Montenegro, we sorely lack qualified forestry engineers, and instead of sending me more people like you, they give you a visa to leave the country! Well, we shall see about that!" he shouted to Vladimir. He then proceeded to place a long-distance call to the office that had issued the exit visa. When he reached that office, he literally screamed into the receiver, "Let me speak to your boss this instant! This is the Minster of Forestry and Agriculture of the People's Republic of Montenegro! What right do you have to issue an exit visa to one of my engineers when we so sorely need them?"

There followed a short conversation, during which comrade minister said several times, "Yes, comrade! Yes, comrade!"

Vladimir had no idea who what "comrade" was, but it seemed that "comrade" greatly outranked the Montenegro minister, who immediately became as docile as a lamb. After hanging up, he politely told Vladimir to go back to Nikshich and pick up his exit visa at the local police office, where it had been confiscated.

CHAPTER 29

Refugees in Italy

American and British aid organizations cooperated in setting up three facilities for refugees in the Free Territory of Trieste from 1947 to 1954. The first, Opicina, consisting of a group of Quonset huts erected in a sweet-smelling pine forest, was devoted to the reception and processing of refugees arriving from Yugoslavia. Valentina's niece, Natasha, worked there as a clerk and interpreter and was waiting with her mother Nina when Valentina arrived with Vladimir and their son Anatole. They were all excited to see each other again and shared an enormous relief to be safely beyond the reach of the Communists and their brutal secret police.

By that time, autumn had arrived and the air was damp and cold. Valentina was given a cot in an unheated hut. The fogs that rolled in off the sea chilled her to the bone, provoking early symptoms of arthritis. Movies were screened several times a week, and USO (United Service Organization) entertainers occasionally came to perform, but Valentina invariably spent her evenings indoors.

The family lived in the Quonset hut at Opicina for two months before being sent on to the second refugee facility San Sabba—a big, aging, red-brick building that had been converted from a rice polishing factory into apartments for refugee families. Under the Nazis, the building had been used as a prison for Communists, Jews, Romanies, and other blacklisted groups of people. Valentina and her family were given a room on the second floor, and sheltered from the fog and cold winds, Valentina's arthritis immediately improved. The walls and pillars on the top floor of the three-story building were scrawled by the inmates; Valentina learned that the inmates who were charged with capital crimes had been confined, and they had scrawled graffiti comments over the walls.

"December 5, 1943, Moshe Weinberg was killed by the fascists."

"I am waiting to be executed. Today is February 11, 1944."

"Brother, if you survive, be happy in the time you have."

Although the Italians had not treated the Jewish prisoners with the unspeakable cruelty that the Germans had, nevertheless, these graffiti messages sent a shiver down Valentina's spine.

For refugees from Communist Yugoslavia, the sight on May Day of Italian Communists, honoring the memory of their fallen comrades who had perished at San Sabba with red banners and floral wreaths, held a measure of déjà vu.

The third facility, San Giusto, housing single men, had served as a prison since Renaissance times and had bars on all its windows. Rumor had it that each time a violent crime was committed in Trieste, the police would go first to San Giusto to round up suspects. Valentina heard that there were occasional reports, too, of knife fights among refugees of different ethnicities (for reasons unfathomable to Valentina) between Hungarians and Bulgarians.

Prison of San Giusto included Greeks, Romanians, Hungarians, Albanians, Serbs, Croats, Bulgarians, and Russians, and a wide sampling of other ethnicities. The majority of internees were, like Valentina, native speakers of Russian who had fled to Trieste from Yugoslavia, where, like Valentina, they had gained fluency in Serbo-Croatian.

Through Natasha's connections with the camp's administrators and Valentina's language ability, Valentina was able to find work as a typist and interpreter for Ms. Claire MacMurray, a tall, red-haired Scottish woman, who had been sent there by the YWCA. For her services, Valentina received a small amount of cash plus food and clothing. For many years thereafter, Valentina corresponded with Ms. MacMurray, who eventually married a Czech refugee she had met at a camp in Austria. The newly weds then immigrated to Australia.

Valentina's work enabled her family to supplement their meals. The camp kitchens provided sufficient nourishment, but the chief nutrients consisted of carbohydrates, a modicum of protein, and vitamins and minerals from a few fresh vegetables. Mostly Valentina ate pasta or bread each day in and day out, with beans and rice for variety. A small portion of ground horsemeat in a thin soup was served once a week on Sunday. Milk was given only to the younger children and the sick. To supplement their meager fare, the family would buy horsemeat hamburgers sold by refugee entrepreneurs who hawked their wares in the corridors.

Each of the three floors of San Sabba consisted of a single large room partitioned off with plywood into narrow apartments. Valentina couldn't see the people living near to her but could hear everything they said or did. All the petty sorrows and joys of each resident's life were open to silent neighborly witness: a husband beating his wife or making love to her, gasps of pain, moans of delight, laughter, or tears. No one possessed any secrets.

There was a place outside the camp building called *Brekhalovka* (Gossiping Place), where the Russians liked to gather and exchange information. One day, at *Brekhlovka*, Valentina heard a US Army sergeant haranguing the loungers at *Brekhalovka* in English. It was still early morning, and besides the American sergeant, Valentina could see only a few elderly Russians in the area. Valentina recognized, among the sergeant's audience, a former White Army general and a Russian Orthodox deacon. She watched the handful of men straining to understand what the American was saying.

"What's the matter with you people?" he drawled. "Why can't you get along with your own countrymen? Why do you want to leave the land of your ancestors? In American politics, the other party sometimes wins. You know. But what can you do? Half of the American population wouldn't leave their homeland just because the party they voted for didn't win the election."

The sergeant paused and chuckled. The Russian men responded with hesitant laughter, and this, in turn, encouraged the sergeant to blunder on. Pointing at the general, he said, "Anyway, why'd you vote for the Communist Party if you don't support it? What do you say to that?"

The general paused to consult his few words of English, then replied, "OK."

"See? Got you there," said the sergeant and sauntered off.

Valentina was astounded by the American sergeant's incredible political ignorance.

But then she considered that the Russian refugees must surely have seemed a strange lot to the American. The first thing the Russians had done when they arrived in this village of transients was to organize an Orthodox church. The next was to start up a theater. After that every Sunday evening, the refugees could watch a variety show held on a stage in the first-floor dining hall. Since the camp housed many talented people, including professional actors and singers, the Sunday shows were often extremely entertaining and were well attended. On nights when there were no performances, the refugees played bingo, which was popular with the elderly.

Valentina's boss, Ms. MacMurray, helped to organize a school for the children, and among her young scholars was the ten-year-old Anatole, one of her young scholars.

Representatives of countries that resettled refugees came to recruit workers for their factories or farms. Some of the delegates from these recruiting missions came from North and South America, as well as from Australia. They treated the refugees like beasts of burden, demanding that the men show them their muscles or teeth. The recruiters poked the refugees' muscles as if they were bartering for horses.

At that time, Valentina and Vladimir were both in their late 40s and had no future as laborers. When Vladimir, after great effort, succeeded in conveying to one delegate that he was a specialist and wanted to work in the field in which he had been trained, he received the curt reply, "We have enough specialists in our country. What we need is good strong muscle."

Vladimir and Valentina both felt disappointed to hear this. It was not so difficult for Valentina who was already using her language skills to earn money in the camp. Vladimir, however, grew bitter because he felt that he was idling away his life.

"This wouldn't have happened if we hadn't left Yugoslavia!" he complained to Valentina. She took this as a reproach directed at her for insisting they emigrate. She responded with anger by throwing a pair of scissors at his feet. Young Anatole witnessed this outburst of anger and was terrified. He had long basked in the warmth of his parents' unwavering love for each other. Now he felt this was threatened.

At last, the day at last arrived when Natasha signed a contract with a Canadian immigration officer under which she agreed to work at a hospital in Toronto. The hospital administration had been unable to find a sufficient number of Canadians to staff its menial positions. Natasha felt the job had a future, so she decided to accept the offer. She assured her mother and aunt that she would make arrangements to bring them over once she had settled in Toronto.

And so Natasha, always the bright-eyed go-getter, went off to Canada to work. Very soon, she had made all the arrangements for Valentina and her family to immigrate to Canada. As agreed, Nina, in turn, would be brought over under the sponsorship of Valentina.

In preparation for their immigration to Canada, Valentina, Vladimir, and Anatole were sent from Trieste to a refugee camp in Bagnoli, near Naples. This was the internment center for those in transit out of Italy. The center was luxurious in comparison to the places where they had previously stayed. Built by Mussolini as an elite officers' training school, its amenities included a sports arena, an outdoor movie theater, and even restaurants.

In order to obtain an immigration visa for Canada, the applicants had to go to Rome and apply to the consul attached to the Canadian Embassy. Hence, Valentina, Vladimir, and Anatole set off by train for Rome.

Unfortunately, their first trip to Rome was not a success. At that time, some Italian medical professionals were engaged in a scheme to sell X-rays. The swindlers would tell a healthy person that he had pulmonary TB, showing him the X-ray of an infected person and then, for a fee, offer to arrange for a second opinion.

One Italian medical practitioner told Vladimir that his X-ray showed a shadow and that Vladimir required a second diagnosis. The doctor even arranged to book a hotel room for the family. However, Vladimir had heard of such schemes and confident that he didn't have TB, so he refused the doctor's offer. Vladimir and Valentina returned to Bagnoli, both empty-handed and with empty pockets.

This was 1951, and at the time, Valentina was working in the Bagnoli office of the International Refugee Organization. She told her colleagues about their misadventure in Rome. One of her Italian colleagues advised her not to mail a second set of X-rays. "Go with them in person," he said, "and never for a moment let the doctor lose sight of your real x-ray."

Thanks to this advice, Valentina, her husband, and her son succeeded in getting their Canadian entry permits on their second trip to Rome. Afterward, they returned to Bagnoli to await a berth on the earliest boat sailing for Canada. In due course, together with a large group of refugees, Valentina and her family boarded a train at Naples, destined for Bremen, a port city on the Weser River in Germany, from where they would later board a US Navy troop transport ship and sail for Canada.

Their train journey from Italy took them through Austria to Germany. Valentina enjoyed conversing with her fellow passengers. They all felt animated by their rosy visions of life in a New World paradise far from war-torn Europe. Of all the places they passed through on the way north, Valentina liked Innsbruck the best. It reminded her so much of Slovenia, where she had spent one of the happiest years of her life.

While waiting for the boat to Canada, they were interned for a month at a refugee facility on the outskirts of Bremen. Here they were free to walk about town at their leisure.

One day, Vladimir went to a confectioner's shop to buy candies for Anatole. Unfamiliar with German currency, however, he paid too much. Only when he returned from shopping did he realize his miscalculation. That upset him considerably. Since only a small sum of money was lost, Valentina urged him to forget it. Vladimir was adamant. He insisted on returning to the store where, after Vladimir explained to him his error, the clerk politely returned the amount due to him. This surprised Valentina, and she decided that Germany was not at all like the undisciplined Italy. Germany had lost the war. Its cities lay in ruins. Its people, however, seemed honest and trustworthy.

CHAPTER 30

To Canada

The crossing from the German port of Bremerhaven to Halifax in Nova Scotia, Canada, took five days. Their ship, the *USS General Sturgis,* with its cargo of refugees, sailed into the harbor at Halifax on September 12, 1951.

As the ship eased its way past the breakwater, Valentina gazed in bewilderment at the barren, rocky shore, dotted here and there with a spattering of tiny houses. Not only were there no skyscrapers, but few of the buildings overlooking the port rose higher even than one single story. The terrain presented a vista at once, boundless and barren, while the sea, in the eyes of one, accustomed to the azure blue of the Adriatic, appeared cold and grey.

Valentina wondered what awaited her here in this newest of her borrowed homelands. She was now nearly fifty and showing early signs of arthritis. Valentina had resigned herself to doing factory work until she became fluent in English.

She hoped that Natasha could help her find a job in Toronto, where Natasha now lived. *From now on, I'll have to live like a Canadian*, she reminded herself, though she was none too certain just what being a Canadian involved.

Valentina and family left Halifax by train headed for Toronto. Natasha had sent tickets and a little money to tide them over until they arrived.

As the train chugged through the Canadian countryside, they became aware of two curious facts. First, it was a cause of concern to Vladimir that no police ever came to check their documents. *How could the Canadians protect their country from Communist spies and saboteurs if they did not check travelers' documents?* The more he thought about it, the more concerned Vladimir became. Finally, he decided that it was a matter of efficiency. *The Royal Canadian Police must have found a way to keep track of each person's movements without the need of constantly checking people's documents!*

The second curious fact was the factory-like buildings they saw. Town after town contained enormous buildings surrounded by huge parking lots packed with cars. At first, Vladimir thought the towns manufactured cars and that the cars parked beside them were waiting to be shipped out. Finally, however, it dawned on him that all these cars belonged to the people who worked in the factories. Life was a series of discoveries, none of which can be explained by any precedent. *What a wealthy country! So many ordinary laborers managing could afford their own cars!* To a postwar European, the notion of a factory worker commuting to work by private vehicle was outside the realm of belief.

The Lyovins would be starting life anew with only the few dollars they had brought with them from Yugoslavia, plus the money Natasha had sent for their final leg of their trip. This was not the first time Valentina had given up all her worldly possessions in order to start life afresh. She had survived the Russian Revolution in Petrograd, the bloody civil war that followed, a typhoid epidemic in southern Russia, the Second World War in Yugoslavia, and most recently, the deprivations of life in a refugee camp. Nevertheless, she pressed on, confident that not only would she and her family survive but that they would steadily improve their lot in life. She felt that their survival thus far was part of an ongoing miracle, surely the result of her deep faith, which never for a moment she had abandoned.

Valentina and family were met at the station in Toronto by a happy, smiling Natasha. As they made their way to their new home, Natasha complained that the hospital representatives she now worked for had not told her that she would be working in a psychiatric hospital. Nonetheless, she did not hesitate to ask Vladimir if he would be willing to work there, too, as a night watchman. It was the only job she had been able to find for him — he spoke even less English than Valentina did; he accepted Natasha's offer. Natasha then took them to the place she had found for them to stay, a spacious room with a shared kitchen.

"It was hard to find a residence for you because of Anatole's age. If you tell a landlord that you have a boy of twelve or thirteen, he will usually reject you," she added. Valentina wondered why this was so. Anatole would soon be twelve, but he had never once caused his family any trouble. Before long, however, she noticed the way the twelve-year-old children in her new host country behaved; then she understood all too well.

Among the many odd things that Vladimir noted about his new homeland was the puzzling question as to why, in such a peaceful country as Canada, there should be what appeared to him to be a disproportionate number of mentally disturbed people. He knew that Canada had been spared the horrors and residual traumas of total war, like the one so mercilessly visited upon combatants in Europe. From a distance, the Canadians had watched Europe disintegrate, but they themselves had never been threatened with the annihilation of their urban populations or with the demolition of their cultural and economic infrastructures. Safe and sound on the other side of the globe, the Canadians had not been compelled to live in the gripping shadow of cold fear.

Another circumstance that perplexed him was the enormous number of senile people among the institutionalized. Why didn't their children care for them?

Vladimir had graduated from the University of Belgrade and had served as a government forestry engineer in Yugoslavia. He wanted a job that his education and training qualified him for. His inability to speak English, however, prevented his attaining such a job. Growing ever more depressed, he began to take his frustrations out on Valentina.

"If you hadn't come up with this ridiculous idea of leaving Yugoslavia, we wouldn't be going through this now!" he bitterly complained to her.

They bickered endlessly. On occasion, Vladimir resorted to violence, and Valentina considered divorcing him. She once asked Anatole which of them he would live with if they divorced, and it startled her to hear him say, "I feel sorry for Papa, so I'd stay with him." Although startled to hear this, Valentina was touched to know that her son felt sorry for his father, who must work at an unpleasant job in order to make a living for the family. Valentina decided that she would not make Anatole live through the tragedy of a divorce.

For Anatole, it was distressing to see his parents suffering, but being young and having a penchant for study, he was soon drawn out of his unhappy situation by books in English that would enable him to excel at school.

Soon after Valentina and her family joined her in Toronto, Natasha married a Serbian engineer named Milan, fifteen years her senior. He warned Valentina that her educated background could work against her, and until she could carry on a conversation in English, the only type of job one could hope to get was one of drudgery. Indeed, she too had considered it inevitable even before she set foot in Canada, and for two years, she sought only jobs requiring physical labor. Milan's prediction came true. Valentina found that, even for a factory job, if she wrote in her application that she was a college graduate, her prospective employer would give her suspicious looks and then turn her down. Next, she wrote that she was a high school graduate, but even this was apparently considered too much education for a factory worker. At a small ceramics factory, she submitted an application, in which she declared herself to have attended only elementary school. The factory owner, out of sympathy for the embarrassment he thought she must feel, assured her that it did not concern him in the least. He then asked her to paint eyebrows on ceramic doll faces. She tried, but her hands shook so much with nervousness that she still didn't get the job.

Natasha's mother Nina was working in a toy factory. Nina arranged with her boss to hire Valentina. The factory was a large and filthy structure—cold and drafty in winter, hot and dusty in summer—with machines running day and night. The majority of workers, as well as the foreman, were Japanese-Canadians, and the rest were Anglo-Canadians. At first, no one spoke to Valentina except for one English woman, who was kind to her and protected her from the often-irascible boss. The factory produced very cheap toys at a time when similar products of better quality were being made even more cheaply in Japan. The foreman and the owner of the factory drove the workers hard and paid them minimal wages to keep production costs competitive.

The experience Valentina gained at this job enabled her to get a marginally better-paying job at a ceramics factory owned by an Italian. She had no problem painting faces on ceramic dolls and designs on cheap lamps there. The room where the imitation Chinese and Japanese dolls were produced was a poorly ventilated cellar, and Valentina found the smell of heated chemicals to be overpowering.

On the days when the government inspector came to assess working conditions, the boss did not heat the chemicals, so the inspector never smelled the noxious fumes. Even the garbage can was cleaned the day before these supposedly unannounced visits. The inspector typically received a big box of gifts from the owner and would go home declaring himself satisfied with the working conditions at the factory.

As Valentina gradually got to know the members of the congregation at the Toronto Russian Orthodox Church, she soon discovered that many Russian women held office jobs despite the fact that their English, in Valentina's view, was not as good as her own. Valentina made up her mind to get herself a proper position in an office.

She attended a bookkeeping class in the evenings, and when she received her certificate, she asked a Canadian couple who were well-connected in the community to help her find an office job. She was thrilled when she was offered a clerical job at the Blue Cross Insurance Company. For the first time since coming to Canada, she began to earn a monthly salary and not an hourly wage.

However, the chief joy for Valentina was that Anatole, who had been a sickly child, was now thriving in Canada. By now he was in high school. He was an avid scholar and did well in school.

In June 1959, Anatole graduated with honors from Bloor Collegiate High School as the valedictorian of his class. Anatole, who, under the Yugoslav Communist regime, would have been denied entrance to a university simply on the grounds of 'belonging to the wrong social class,' had been offered scholarships at both the University of Toronto and at Princeton University in the United States. He chose Princeton. He wanted to leave home and be free from his parents.

Valentina considered that her decision to come to Canada had been redeemed in full by Anatole's academic success. For Vladimir, however, the deep satisfaction he gained from his son's achievement was, perhaps, even more heartfelt because of the immense cost to Vladimir's own self-respect. He never got over having to abandon his own career as a forestry engineer in Yugoslavia.

Vladimir often told Anatole that the godless Communist regime would fall sooner or later. "This regime cannot stay in this world. It will fall for sure. I won't be around to see it, but you, my son, will see it." This prediction of Vladimir's would come true in 1991.

CHAPTER 31

The New Member of the Family

In the early years of my marriage into this Russian family, I was very much aware of my Japanese "foreign" status. By the year 1966, I felt I had already entered into the lives of the Lyovin family. It took only a few years to become a daughter to Valentina and mother to Anatole's son. I was just another member of the Lyovin household.

The biggest event in my early days as a member of the Lyovin family was the death of my father-in-law. On March 7, 1966, Vladimir reported as usual to his superior in the hospital where he worked as a night watchman. After finishing his rounds, he was told he could leave, but he did not respond. A massive heart attack had carried him off in an instant at the age of sixty-two. We buried Vladimir at the Russian Orthodox Monastery in Jordanville, New York, a five hours' drive by car from Toronto. Valentina did not weather the death of her husband at all well. They had quarreled the evening before he left for his last night at work. Valentina felt a twinge of remorse over not having been pleasanter to her husband. The quarrel was over his retirement and his wish to live with us.

Valentina blamed Anatole for not promising them that they could live with us.

One week after Vladimir's funeral, Valentina also suffered a heart attack. She too was sixty-two years old. As a result, she retired from her position at the Ontario Insurance Company and headed for Berkeley, California, in the hopes of renting a big house, where all of us could live together. Her hope could not be realized, however, since we had just rented a two-bedroom apartment in the Cal University Village. Valentina ended up renting a studio apartment in Berkeley for only a year.

When I had first met Valentina, shortly after my arrival in San Francisco in 1964, we had flown to Chicago to visit Olga's son, Dmitry, and his family. On the plane to Chicago, Valentina asked me what the custom in Japan was regarding caring for aged parents. I replied that usually the eldest son lived with the parents and took care of them. I sensed that she did not like this answer and that she wanted me to tell her that I would like for her to live with Anatole and me.

Dmitry had completed medical school in Vienna before emigrating to the United States, where he served as an army doctor, later taking a position as an anesthesiologist at a hospital in Chicago. I met Dmitry, his wife, and their two daughters. They were living in a spacious house in an affluent residential area in Western Springs outside Chicago.

Dmitry's mother Olga, Valentina's brother Modest's wife, happened to be living in San Francisco with her second husband. Modest and his family had left Yugoslavia soon after the Nazi occupation and were living in Vienna during the war. In 1950, they emigrated to the United States and settled in Bogalusa, Louisiana. However, Modest, a trained engineer, could not find suitable work in Louisiana and decided to move to Indiana. In 1951, Modest died suddenly from a heart attack after driving with his family from Louisiana all the way to Indiana. The long trip through unfamiliar territory may have been too exhausting for him.

After his death, Olga developed a dependency on alcohol, though she was able to refrain from the drink after marrying an Armenian architect, Leon Hovanesian, with whom she now lived in a neat Victorian-style house in San Francisco, which I visited with Valentina.

I sensed a deep resentment in Valentina toward this man. I later learned that back in Yugoslavia, Leon had been a tenant of Modest and Olga. Valentina suspected them of cuckolding her brother Modest. Nonetheless, Valentina wanted to see Olga, with whom she had faced great hardship and mortal danger during the civil war.

Olga died in 1975 in San Francisco. By coincidence, Valentina just happened to be in California at the time. Anatole was then on sabbatical leave from the University of Hawaii, and so we could stay for a year in California. Valentina felt that some mystic power had arranged for her to be near Olga when she died.

I had always liked Olga for her kind heart. She came to help Anatole and me when our son Nicholas was born in Berkeley.

In Toronto, I met Valentina's niece, Natasha, and her family. They were living in a huge three-story brick house they had bought together with Valentina's family. Natasha pioneered the immigration route to Toronto that brought Valentina's family to the New World. She was, like her aunt Valentina, a gifted linguist, but she also possessed an unfailing instinct for a good business deal.

Natasha was a good-looking, confident middle-aged working woman. She once told me while on a shopping excursion, "Back in the days when I was a miserable refugee in Trieste, Italy, I used to watch the rich American tourists who were staying at the best hotels. They could buy anything they wanted at the drop of a hat. I vowed that one day I would travel like that."

Sharp-minded Natasha got better and better positions, and though she married and started a family, she stayed on the job while her mother Nina took care of her three children. With the money she earned, she bought one property after another; in the meantime, she also got a college degree in accounting and became a licensed tax auditor. Thirty years later, she traveled as a tourist through Italy and Yugoslavia, staying at the best hotels in fulfillment of her worldly vow.

In 1968, two years after Vladimir's death, Valentina left her home in Toronto and moved to Honolulu to be with us. Enchanted by the island lifestyle, Valentina fell in love with the Hawaiian dress called the *muumuu*. I knew how to sew, so I sewed many *muumuus* for her. Valentina looked very elegant in the long formal *muumuus*, but she requested patch pockets on the less formal everyday *muumuus*. For the better *muumuus*, I made hidden pockets. Much later, I understood why she liked to have patch pockets—she liked to carry a collection of necessary items in her pockets, with her around the house at all times.

People she came in contact with were impressed by her polyglot knowledge of European languages. Soon after she arrived, she ran an advertisement in the local newspaper, offering "tutoring in Russian, French, and German." As always, her first concern upon settling into a new home, in a new land, was to find a job. There were several responses to the ad right away; among them were a female sociology professor, a somewhat eccentric millionaire who owned a farm in Waimanalo and kept horses, a Honolulu Circuit Court judge who planned to travel to the Soviet Union, and a Greek Orthodox priest who wanted to learn Russian because he had many Russian parishioners. She had hardly arrived and already had gathered a coterie of admiring students, all wanting her to teach them Russian. I was impressed as I watched her expertly converse with her circle of sharp intellectuals.

Valentina gave much of her time to her grandsons, Nicholas and Andrei. She spoke to her grandsons only in Russian, in the hopes they would use the language someday. The elder grandson, Nicholas, later married a Russian girl from St. Petersburg, while the younger one, Andrei, was able to use his Russian tongue for his advanced degree in psychology.

Valentina used to say to me, "I hate stingy people!" and was generous with what little money she had. Throughout her life, she had encountered many wealthy penny-pinchers who made the worship of money the central focus of their lives. She thought it ridiculous to cling so tightly to something which cannot be taken into the other world.

Because Valentina had lost everything twice in her life—once because of the Russian Revolution and again when she left Yugoslavia for the free world—she lived a simple life and bought only what she needed. Yet she was very easy about spending. "I have worked all my life, so I am not afraid of spending my money," she often said. In this respect, she loved shopping for her family or friends. Indeed, an attitude of faith surrounded her feelings about money. Whenever she ran out of money, more would somehow turn up from somewhere. Valentina would then smile and say, "The Lord takes care of the money."

Valentina was a tasteful dresser and neat in her personal habits. She loved to use a brand of soap manufactured by the Avenin Company in Germany because the floral fragrances brought back memories of Europe.

There was no Russian Orthodox Church in Honolulu when we arrived, so the family joined the congregation of Sts. Constantine and Helen Greek Orthodox Church. Valentina would dress for church in a simple black dress with a string of pearls, and the natural grace of her tall figure and slender legs would, on more than one occasion, lead people to suppose that she was an exiled Russian noblewoman.

Valentina, tossed on the waves of violent historical events, was thrice married and twice compelled to emigrate by repressive Communist regimes, but never did she lose the aura of one blessed and protected by her strong Russian Orthodox faith. These hardships throughout her life had helped Valentina to grow spiritually. I respected and greatly admired the way she lived.

CHAPTER 32

Valentina's Twilight Years

In the fall of 1978, ten years after Valentina had come to live with us in Hawaii, Anatole was offered a Fulbright professorship at the Korea University in Seoul. He accepted, and I invited Valentina to come to Korea with our family. She told us that she did not want to go to another foreign country at her age, which by then had arrived at seventy-six years old. Instead, she chose to live with her elder son Boris in Sacramento, California. She knew there were a fine Russian Orthodox Church and excellent medical facilities near Boris's house. In 1982, she underwent heart bypass surgery at the nearby facilities. However, she missed her grandsons very much and insisted on visiting us in Hawaii every winter.

Following her recovery from her bypass surgery, Valentina embarked on a project of great importance to her. She wrote an English translation of *Macarius of Optina*, a compilation of the insights of Macarius, founder of the tradition of eldership at Optina Monastery in Russia. The Russian original had been published by Tip V. Gote of Moscow in 1861.

At the time of its origin in the mid-nineteenth century, the *startsy* (elders) of the Optina Monastery had attracted spiritual seekers, including such literary luminaries as Dostoevsky, Tolstoy, and Gogol. The *startsy* served as charismatic spiritual leaders, whose wisdom was said to stem from ascetic communion with the Holy Spirit. The *startsy* were believed to have the power to penetrate a person's heart and discern God's plan for that person's life. Valentina recalled that her father Valerian had planned to make the pilgrimage to Optina, which was located some 180 miles southwest of Moscow.

The Communists had closed and dismantled the monastery in 1923, but it was reopened in 1987 shortly before the fall of the Soviet Union. Valentina felt this would be her last mission to translate one volume of the wisdom of these saintly monks for the benefit of English-speaking seekers. She had met many Americans who had been seriously looking for the "true faith," and she wanted to help those thirsty souls.

Valentina began to undertake this task in 1983 when she was eighty-one years old. She completed the translation in 1993. Her work was published by the St. Herman Brotherhood Press in 1995 under the title *Elder Macarius of Optina*, volume three of the Optina Elders Series.

Mikhail Gorbachev's *Perestroika* reforms of 1985 had set in motion a process ended in the breaching of the Berlin Wall on November 11, 1989. This culminated in the displacement of Communism in Europe.

At long last, with the increasing institutionalization of *Perestroika*, it became possible to correspond freely with Soviet citizens without fear of repercussions. The eighty-eight-year-old Valentina took this opportunity to write a letter to the magazine *Aurora*, published in Leningrad. The letter appeared in the November 1990 issue under the heading "A Letter from Sacramento" and included her postal address.

The letter read as follows:

Dear Brothers and Sisters,

I recently read with great interest that the citizens of Leningrad were contemplating the reinstatement of former place names and that the opinions of Russians living abroad would be taken into consideration. Well, here is my vote for changing Peace Square back to the original Hay Market Square ("Sennaya Ploshchad").

I was born a daughter of a priest, Father Valerian Fedotovich Borotinski, who served for several years at the Uspensky Church (also called "Savior on the Sennaya") until 1917.

My family and I lived in quarters across from the church, where there were many splendid icons donated by wealthy merchants. I remember that some of the icons were decorated with priceless jewels, and that two sentries stood watch at night.

Although I am uncertain what weight my vote for restoration of the name Sennaya Square will carry, I nevertheless beg to inform you of my further wish that a new church be built to replace the one that was demolished to make way for Sennaya Metro Station.

Valentina Valerianovna Lyovin

Among the dozen or so responses that Valentina received was a letter from a middle-aged woman named Evgenia, who asked, "Are you by any chance a relative of mine? Your maiden name is the same as my grandfather's, and it's a very rare one in Russia." Evgenia later wrote that not only did her grandfather have the same last name as Valentina's father but that he, too, had been a clergyman.

In 1991, Valentina suffered a stroke and entrusted her correspondence to Anatole. Subsequently, Evgenia sent him an oil portrait of her great-grandfather Fedot. It now became clear that Evgenia's grandfather was a brother of Valentina's father. Valentina was overjoyed to learn that a cousin of hers had survived the turmoil of the Communist era. Moreover, although Valentina had been told that her grandfather was a church reader, it was now clear from information recorded on the reverse side of the picture, painted in 1878, that Fedot had later been ordained as a deacon.

After suffering a stroke, Valentina could not walk by herself. It was arranged for her to enter a nursing home near Boris's home, where she would have twenty-four-hour care. Boris and Helen visited Valentina daily, sometimes twice a day. Even after Valentina suffered more strokes, her mind remained lucid, and it seemed filled with great excitement. It was at the nursing home that Valentina heard the news of the fall of the Soviet Union, the godless regime. She watched the unfolding drama on her TV. She followed each report on the breakup of both the Soviet Union and Yugoslavia. With a mixture of joy and bitterness, she witnessed the great changes sweeping Russia. She commented on every new event that transpired in her beloved native land. "So there is no more Communism, no more Russian Revolution!" she retorted.

"And after all the mayhem and so many deaths." She shook her head. "What was it all about?" Valentina could not stop her tears. She remembered the prediction of her late husband, Vladimir. "The godless regime cannot survive too long."

Valentina's letter to the editor had developed into another regular correspondence, mediated by Anatole, with a young woman named Alyona. Alyona was studying Indonesian at the University of Leningrad. Her name had been added to a list of people that our son Nicholas planned to meet during a forthcoming visit to Russia. That year, Nicholas had quit his job in San Francisco and took a summer immersion course in Russian language at Middlebury College in Vermont. He wanted to witness with his own eyes the historical events taking place in Russia.

In October 1992, Nicholas visited St. Petersburg, which had shed the name Leningrad and reverted to its old name. Nicholas and Alyona met and fell in love. Nicholas proposed to Alyona on their second date. Following the ceremony in October 1993, the two went to Valentina's nursing home to announce their marriage and receive Valentina's blessings.

During the two years and nine months she spent at the nursing home, Valentina never lost her air of gentility and intelligence, and she was always neatly groomed.

Anatole and I visited Valentina every summer to give Boris and his wife Helen a break from their caretaking responsibilities. Valentina could be difficult at times, and there were many conflicts between her and Boris and Helen. In one instance, she abruptly informed us that she had fallen in love with a fellow resident in the nursing home.

"I got married for the fourth time," she announced.

Boris asked around and learned that there was, in fact, no record of a marriage. But in her heart, Valentina was forever young and in love, and she insisted that her children accept as truth what was true for her, and they did.

"Mama, which of your four husbands have you loved the most?" I asked impudently.

"Oh, Robert, of course!" came the unhesitating reply.

One day, during our summer visit, Valentina asked me to take her to the nearby state-run Indian museum. She was suddenly interested in the place, and as I pushed her wheelchair through the museum, I wondered why.

I found out that her would-be husband, Robert, was an American Indian. Valentina seemed to know a great deal about Robert with who she had apparently spent many a warm, California afternoon in congenial conversation. Through these conversations, she developed a deep and loving respect. Robert, who suffered from diabetes, was removed from the home to the parent medical facility to have his leg amputated. He never came back. In his absence, Valentina refused to eat or take her medicine.

Valentina closed her eventful ninety-two-year life on June 20, 1994, at Sutter Oak Nursing Center in Sacramento. On the day she lapsed into a coma, Boris and his wife Helen stayed with her until 10:00 p.m. However, her doctor told them that her condition was likely to continue unchanged for another twenty-four hours, and so they went home to get some rest. In the small hours, there came a phone call from the Nursing Center, informing them that Valentina had passed away peacefully at two o'clock that morning.

The funeral service was presided over by Father Pavel Volmensky, Valentina's longtime confessor, at the Russian

Orthodox Church of the Ascension in Sacramento. Her coffin was placed in the middle of the church surrounded by an elegant display of mostly white flowers. The choir sang several beautiful and solemn chants. Then Father Pavel intoned the words "Memory Eternal," which were three times chanted by the choir while he circled her coffin, swinging his censer.

The deacon read, "Grant rest eternal in blessed repose, Oh Lord, unto thy servant Valentina who has fallen asleep, and make her memory to be eternal." Then the choir sang "Memory Eternal" three times to a crescendos. This deeply affecting Russian Orthodox funeral service brought a fitting closure to a long life lived straight from the heart.

The burial took place immediately afterward at the nearby Russian Orthodox Cemetery. Valentina had made the arrangements for her funeral years in advance. In July 1994, just a month after Valentina passed away, a baby girl, eventually baptized as Valentina in honor of her great grandmother Valentina, was born to Nicholas and Alyona.

One year later, when the soil had settled over her grave, a marble headstone was erected. The fee for the gravestone was almost the exact sum remaining in Valentina's account.

EPILOGUE

Valentina's sister, Sania, who in 1950 had emigrated to Brazil with her husband and daughter Xenia, lived to see her hundredth birthday in the year 2000. Surviving all her siblings, she must surely have been surrounded by a loving and reverent family to have reached such a ripe old age.

Four years before Anatole had retired from his position as professor of linguistics at the University of Hawaii, he donned his priest robes. He was ordained a Russian Orthodox priest at the Cathedral of Joy for All Who Sorrow at San Francisco on July 28, 1998. It would have given his mother great joy to have learned that she, Valentina, had become not only the daughter of a priest but the mother of a priest as well. She would surely have smiled to know that I too had become now — *matushka* of her beloved church.

ACKNOWLEDGMENTS

Valentina could never have been finished without the help of those people who worked with me during my long struggle with English, my second language.

I have been blessed with many generous and talented friends who aided me in putting together this English version of *Valentina*.

First, I thank David Dutcher for major editing. For gathering data on Russia and for their generous cooperation, I thank Patricia Polansky of the University of Hawaii at Manoa's Hamilton Library and Harold Leich of the European Section at the Library of Congress in Washington DC.

I am indebted to the following people for reading my work with a critical eye: Steve Wagenseller, Travis Summersgill, Jean Geil, Karen Calogeras, Nellie McLaughlin, Anya Pitzer, Hank Chapin, Carol Shimokawa, Father Paul and Matushka Gabrielle Burholt, Allison Schaefers, Joann Otineru, John Belt, Jacqueline Chun, Bill Ridgeway, my granddaughter Valentina Lyovin, and all my colleagues who attended Joe Tsujimoto's writer's workshop at the Punahou School in Honolulu.

A special thanks goes to His Eminence Kyrill of the San Francisco Russian Orthodox Cathedral for giving me valuable advice on Chapter 3, Pascha.

My heartfelt gratitude goes to the New York-based illustrator, Hiro Kimura for his tireles work in creating the beautiful cover.

Last but not least, I would like to express my thanks to my husband, Father Anatole, who served as my ready-reference walking encyclopedia for all things under the warm Hawaiian sun.

Emiko Lyovin
Honolulu
Pascha 2012

BIBLIOGRAPHY

Andrews, Peter. *The Rulers of Russia.* Chicago: Stonehenge Press Inc., 1979.

Brinkley, George A. *The Volunteer Army and Allied Intervention in South Russia, 1917-1921.* Notre Dame, Indiana: University of Notre Dame Press, 1966.

Denikine, Anton Ivanovich. *The White Army:* Westport, Connecticut: Hyperion Press, Inc., 1973.

Erickson, Crolly. *Alexandra The Last Tsarina.* New York: St. Martin's Griffin

Fedotov, George P. *A Treasury of Russian Spirituality.* Belmont, Massachusetts: Nordland Publishing Company, 1975.

FitzLyon, Kyril. Before the revolution, The Overlook Press, 1978

Kenez, Peter. *Civil War in South Russia, 1919-1920.* Berkeley: University of California Press, 1977.

Lehovich, Dimitry. *White against Red.* New York: Norton & Co., Inc., 1994.

Lovell, James Blair. *Anastasia: the Lost Princess.* New York: Regnery Gateway, 1991.

Lyons, Marvin. *Nicholas II: the Last Tsar.* New York: St. Martin's Press, 1974.

Martin, John Stuart.ed. *A Picture History of Russia.* New York: Crown Publishers, Inc., 1968.

Massie, Robert K. *Nicholas and Alexandra.* New York: Dell Publishing Co.,Inc., 1971.

Massie, Robert K. *The Romanovs: the Final Chapter*. New York: Random House, 1995.

Massie, Suzanne. *Land of the Firebird*. New York: Simon and Schuster, 1980.

McDowell, Bart. Journey Across Russia The Soviet Union Today. Washington D.C. National Geographic Society,1977

Mukhin, Vyacheslav. *The Church Culture of Saint Petersburg*. St.Petersburg: Ivan Fyodorov Publishers, 1994.

Obolensky, Chloe. The Russian Empire. New York: Random House, 1979

Ometev, Boris, and John Stuart. *St.Petersburg*. New York: The Vendôme Press, 1990.

Parker, W.H. *An Historical Geography of Russia*. London: University of London Press Ltd., 1968

Pavlovich, Paul. *The Serbians*. Toronto: Serbian Heritage Books, 1983.

Pipes, Richard,ed. *The Russian Intelligentsia*. New York: Colombia University Press, 1961.

Radzinsky, Edward. *The Last Tsar*. New York: Doubleday, 1992.

Salisbury, Harrison E. *Black Night, White Snow: Russia's Revolutions*. New York: Doubleday, 1977.

Schakovskoy, Princess Zinaida. *The Privilege Was Mine*. London: Jonathan Cape Ltd., 1959.

Singleton, Fred. *Twentieth-Century Yugoslavia*. New York: Colombia University Press, 1976.

Steveni, William Barnes. *Petrograd, Past and Present*. London: Grant Richards Ltd., 1915.

West Rebecca. *Black Lamb and Grey Falcon*. 2 vols. New York: The Viking Press, 1941.

Youssoupoff, Prince Felix. *Lost Splendor*. New York: G.P.Putnam's Sons, 1954.

Антонов, В. В., и А. В. Кобак. *Святыни Санкт-Петербурга. Историко-церковная энциклопедия в трех томах.*

Санкт-Петербург: Издательство Чернышева, 1996.

Шульц мл., С. *Храмы Санкт-Петербурга: история и современность.* Санкт-Петербург: «Глаголь», 1994.

Andorich, Ivo. *Dorina no hashi.* Tokyo: Kōbunsha, 1966.

Hara T. *Roshia.* Tokyo: Shinchōsha, 1994.

Kawamata K. *Nikorai no tō.* Tokyo: Chūō Kōron, 1992.

Shiba N. *Yuugosurabia gendai-shi.* Tokyo: Iwanami Shoten, 1996.

Shiba R. *Sakanoue no kumo.* Tokyo: Bungei Shunjū, 1978.

ABOUT THE AUTHOR

Emiko Lyovin was born in 1941 in Tokyo, Japan. After graduating from Sophia University she married Valentina's youngest son Anatole Lyovin, who taught linguistics at the University of Hawaii at Manoa. Just before he retired, Anatole was ordained as a Russian Orthodox priest.

After 28 years of teaching Japanese at Hawaii's prestigious private institution Punahou School, Emiko retired. She lives in Honolulu and now serves as Father Anatole's matushka at his church in Honolulu.